What Worries Parents Most

MARLIN MADDOUX

HARVEST HOUSE PUBLISHERS
Eugene, Oregon 97402

Except where otherwise indicated, all Scripture quotations in this book are taken from the Holy Bible, New International Version, Copyright © 1973, 1978, 1984 by the International Bible Society. Used by permission of Zondervan Bible Publishers.

The names of certain persons mentioned in this book have been changed in order to protect the privacy of the individuals involved.

WHAT WORRIES PARENTS MOST

Copyright © 1992 by Marlin Maddoux
Published by Harvest House Publishers
Eugene, Oregon 97402

Library of Congress Cataloging-in-Publication Data

Maddoux, Marlin.
  What worries parents most / Marlin Maddoux.
  ISBN 0-89081-933-5
  1. Parenting—United States.   2. Child rearing—United States.
3. Child rearing—Religious aspects—Christianity.   4. Social role—United
States.   I. Title
HQ755.8.M33   1992
649′.1—dc20   91-47933
                                                                            CIP

Printed in the United States of America.

CONTENTS

Good News Tent Sale

One McDonld

4-1-96

Part Four
FINISHING WELL

Part
One

WHEN LOVE ISN'T ENOUGH

CHAPTER ONE

The Future: Up for Grabs

Have you noticed it too?

A lot of people have been paying close attention to your children and grandchildren lately. They've been taking a very special interest in them—a little too much interest, if you ask me. And quite often it is the wrong people, with the wrong ideas.

Politicians, educators, journalists, theologians, rock stars, sports heroes, actors and comedians, youth workers, sex deviants, abortionists, lobbyists, and a slew of others are the players who, at one time or another, compete with parents and family to shape the future of a child. The competition is stiff and the stakes are high. Life or death, joy or endless regret, pride or shame, and even your child's eternal destiny hang in the balance.

Million-Dollar Seduction

If you're looking for specifics, entertainers and the entertainment industry are good examples of "the wrong kind of people." The music industry is one that has your child in its sights.

Let's face it: Music producers are *successfully* wooing your kids, seducing them with the likes of Madonna Louise Veronica Ciccone.

Madonna was raised in a typical Roman Catholic home in Pontiac, Michigan, just outside Detroit. In her junior year of high school she abruptly dropped out of cheerleading and began spending time around gay bars in the area. In 1979 the strikingly attractive Madonna starred in her first movie, a thinly veiled porn flick in which her character alternately dominated men and was raped by them.[1]

That was about the time her singing career took off.

Today Madonna can be found donning a crucifix, simulating masturbation on stage, and performing a striptease in front of a stadium teeming with tens of thousands of children aged 9 to 17, or in front of an immense "secondary market" of boys and girls even younger, sitting at home watching one of their idol's 36 videos or two feature-length concerts on MTV.

Madonna is the leading role model for pre-college-age girls in this country today.

Little boys are taught to yearn for a girl just like Madonna. And little girls? Well, they want to dress (and perhaps someday undress) just like Madonna. And the fashion industry knows just how to help them do it.

Saturday Mind Control

Television executives are another good example of the wrong kind of people—executives such as Ted Turner, head of Turner Broadcasting Systems, and *Time* Magazine's 1991 "Man of the Year."

As a child, Ted was raised in a strict Christian home where objectionable kinds of entertainment were discouraged. According to his own account, he rejected his professed faith when his sister was stricken with an agonizing and ultimately fatal illness. As Ted reflected on this crisis, he considered that his Sunday school teachers had given him no way to reconcile their God with what he saw as meaningless and unredeemable suffering. Rather than choosing to seek God in response to the hard questions of life and death, Ted walked away from the church and never looked back, except to sneer.

Today, as one of the most influential media tycoons in America, Ted has presented major speeches attacking the Christian faith as "a religion for losers," has issued his own revised version of the Ten Commandments, and has loudly proclaimed that anyone who adopts a pro-life position on abortion is a "bozo" and an "idiot."

In fact, after turning against the Christian faith, he wants to do all he can to prevent any child from suffering through a "backward" upbringing like his own. Perhaps that's why he and his network created "Captain Planet."

The message of this popular children's cartoon, carefully ornamented with top-notch animation and exciting plot lines, is that free-market America is the enemy, radical environmentalists the heroes, and New Age globalism is the ideal world future. As we shall see, this is a common—and highly successful—children's programming theme.

Ted Turner and many other talented, creative, and dedicated people are paying close attention to your children's desires and needs.

My question to you is this: How closely are your children or grandchildren, your neighbor's children, and the kids in your church paying attention to Ted Turner and similar televangelists—missionaries who have declared your living room to be the field for their undercover humanistic crusades?

Target for Conquest

Make no mistake—high-powered individuals and organizations are working overtime to do reconstructive surgery on your kids' minds and hearts.

This is a fact I live with daily. For one thing, I love children. I've raised four of my own, and now I must lie awake at night with my thoughts tugging back to my grandchildren and the increasingly trip-wired world through which they must somehow find their way. And I've dedicated my life to helping them, as well as your kids.

In the morning when I enter my office, I and my staff at "Point of View" Radio Talk Show seem hardly able to investigate a current event or social issue that doesn't come back to the war for our children.

Children, you see, have become *targets*—like prize territory in savage ground combat. To fight effectively you'll need the right perspective. You'll need to see the battle as something other than a futile bout against unfathomable "social forces," many of which may seem as unmovable as the weather, better left to "the experts."

But always remember that as a parent *you are the expert*. That's why I hope you'll find this book to be more than just an interesting examination of vague forces out there.

I won't beat around the bush: This is a book about the enemy—yours, mine, and our children's.

Observing a new wave of barbarianism sweeping our society, Charles Colson states:

> Unprincipled men and women, disdainful of their moral heritage and skeptical of truth itself, are destroying our civilization by weakening the very pillars on which it rests.[2]

Social forces are begun and kept alive by individuals who make personal decisions. Many of these decisions impact not only their lives but the lives of other people as well. The social forces which threaten to warp our children's values, pervert their behavior, and destroy their future are no different. Whether acting out of malevolence or naivete, *people* are responsible.

Who will prevail? Whose values and behavior will our children decide to adopt? Whose *should* they adopt? Madonna's? Captain Planet's? Yours? How can you keep your child from being engulfed in the crusades of the wrong people as we plunge toward the second half of the 1990's? An uninformed or careless answer could spell disaster, or even death, for your child.

More than ever, parents need to be alert to the dangers and highly aware of the guidelines and resources for effectively counterattacking these enemies.

That's why this book is in your hands, and that's why it's urgent that you read its pages now.

CHAPTER TWO

Winning the Deadliest Battle

There are only two lasting things we give our children—one is roots, the other is wings[1]
—Anonymous

Competition is the mark of America.

In grade school we compete for spelling ribbons and Little League trophies. A bit later we compete for places on the sports team, class honors, scholarships, and attention from the prettiest girl or most handsome guy we know.

And after that? Well, everyone knows what happens next. We keep competing, of course. We compete for jobs, money, market share, praise, homes, cars, a safe neighborhood, a better microwave.

But competition is both a blessing and a curse. It is the engine that drives America, and it is also the grind that sometimes runs us down. Yet the one thing we never thought we'd have to compete for was our own children. We were wrong.

Today the competition for our children is stiff and getting stiffer. Educators are after their minds. Entertainers and athletes are after their devotion. Advertisers are after their money. Politicians are after their loyalties. Ultimately, all of these are after their future, and all can be used by Satan to spiritually destroy them and control the world.

The good news? *This is a competition we can win.* Our children *can* be influenced to avoid the snares of poverty, strife, foolishness, and premature death. And the rewards both on earth and in heaven will be great for those parents who diligently run the course. What does it take to win?

I'll tell you right now, love isn't enough. I've seen too many loving, caring, responsible Christian parents have years of labor and affection blown out of the water when "the competition" gets hold of their son or daughter. Most of the time it is competition they never even knew existed.

Gone are the days when we could smugly hibernate behind the doors of our homes and our churches. The culture kicked in those doors long ago. Today a more aggressive approach is called for. Today we will only preserve our kids by facing the culture as a family—and going on the attack.

It's a new war today, calling for a new battle plan. What worked for your parents and grandparents won't be enough for the task you face today. You may not have to work much harder, but you *will* have to work smarter.

So how do you get started?

The Roots of Home

Kids used to spell relief "F-A-M-I-L-Y." The family was once a safe haven from the bumps, bruises, and blisters of growing up. But today the family is becoming more a *source* of stress than a relief from it. Not only do we have the problems of broken homes, but even in stable homes the extreme career strain of the bread-winners may be alienating children from the experience of putting down healthy roots and building strong relationships. Whether the problem is marital strife or parental preoccupation, the American home is becoming less a safe harbor than a nasty shoreline of hazardous reefs.

Parents, don't let it happen. Make your marriage a priority. *Work on it. Do whatever it takes to make your relationship one of open love, respect, and communication.* And after you've done that, direct that same attention toward your children. Your marriage and family relationships literally form the ship in which your children are floating, and the water is infested with sharks.

For single parents, all is not lost. More work is involved, but it will pay off. It is essential to make use of a close, supportive church and friends. Without a spouse, you must use your extended actual and spiritual family to build a relational "nest" for your children.

Alert to the Warfare

There's no getting around it: Parents are shepherds, and children are sheep. Co-shepherds include grandparents, uncles and aunts, pastors and youth leaders, and virtually any adult.

But in today's America the "shepherds" have more to worry about than ever before. That's because our society is filled with wolves who want to steal and kill our sheep—spiritually, mentally, and often physically. It is my deepest conviction that only those parents who, like the biblical model of the shepherd, are alert to the predators will see their children come through this decade intact.

In this book we will give you an "aerial reconnaissance" of 12 of the most crucial battles you will fight, or that you may be fighting right now. These include:

Battles of behavior:
    Violence, greed, and disrespect
    Ignorance and laziness
    Sexual anarchy
    Homosexuality
    Pornography and sexual perversion
    Drug and alcohol abuse
    Suicide
Battles of belief:
    Cults
    Political seduction
    Secular humanism
    New Age occultism
    Satanism

The fields on which these battles will be fought include entertainment, education, peers, the news media, religion, the streets, your own home, and more. But whatever the battle or battlefield, there are really only three strategic options from which you can choose—options you need to know very well. These are:

1. Protection
2. Preparation
3. Reclamation

Every parent faces day-to-day situations where one or a combination of these options is called for. Which you select will depend on you, your child, and the circumstances. Yet these three options should always be on the mind of parents, who will need them to compete in this fast-paced and dangerous decade. Let's take a closer look at each option.

The Cornerstone

Protection is the cornerstone. Would you let a year-old toddler unwittingly stray into the street? Of course not! The same is true spiritually and morally. Before the age where children can be gradually taught to protect themselves, adults must assume vigilant watch over them. In the chapters that follow, be alert to the dangers which call for protection. Whenever possible I will give my personal recommendations, but many times you will need to make your own judgment call based on your own family's situation, your estimation of your child's maturity, and other factors as well.

True Preparation

The state of alert to which I seek to call parents does not mean a paranoid or hysterical attitude where fear rules your life, and ultimately your child's. I know parents like this, and I feel sorry for their children. Most often these kids become so alienated and suffocated that they rebel at the first chance they get.

Instead of isolation, your response to the threats that menace your children should be 1) full protection while they are still too weak to defend themselves, while at the same time 2) training them to develop a mature Christian character so that they can defend themselves as soon as possible.

Rather than isolation, *insulation* is the key. I'm calling for what youth expert David Wyrtzen (*Raising Worldly-wise But Innocent Kids*, Moody Press) refers to as the "learn and live" approach. In this system for rearing "worldly-wise but innocent kids," a child is trained under the supervision of his parents to perceive good from evil in every area of life as he or she grows. This technique is as old as the book of Proverbs, where a parent is shown giving his son a tour of the world's evils and pointing out the consequences.

According to Wyrtzen, the extremes to avoid are the "live and let learn" school of child-rearing, and the equally harmful error of overprotectionism. "Live and let learn" is the philosophy which sends children unequipped into the school of hard knocks. In today's world of free sex, AIDS, traffic fatalities, and crack, "live and let learn" often means death. On the other hand, secluding your child from the world will only delay his inevitable contact with it—contact which he will not be ready for. When it comes, it could be a fatal collision.

A biblical example of the proper method is found in Proverbs chapter 7. There we see a parent exposing his son to the snare of prostitution while the son is still under parental control and supervision. The parent doesn't isolate the son, setting him up to be blindsided by passion at some future date. Instead, the parent points out step-by-step the methods of the adulteress and prostitute: how she operates, what she will say, when she will strike, the consequences of succumbing, and most important of all, how to resist this kind of temptation.

As you read about the snares to your children described in these pages, think about ways to prepare your child. Jot them down in the margins. Your action today (or failure to act) could literally determine the future of your child.

Opening the Lines

Successful preparation swings on the hinge of successful communication. That means building a relationship with your child as the "make-or-break" link in your strategy. If the link is weak, your strategy will fail, because you are competing for the trust of your child with the future "friends" that he or she will meet.

These "friends" include drug-pushers, boyfriends or girlfriends with mischief on their minds, all kinds of buddies that you will never meet, and every media role model your child will ever have. Who will he or she listen to? Whose advice will he trust? The answer begins now—with your relationship. Put the time in. Work on it.

Winning the Worldview War

Opening lines of communication not only keeps you in touch with your child and builds bonds of emotional affection, but it also allows you to pour into your child the knowledge of God's truth, the insight to integrate it into his or her daily thoughts and actions, and the mental toughness to stick with it when challenged by opposing worldviews.

The Bible presents us with more than a set of dry, esoteric doctrines. It contains a coherent system of looking at *all* areas of life, not just some "religious" or "spiritual" compartments. You need to learn this worldview yourself, to live it in front of your children, and to teach it to them as they grow. Don't be a "functional liberal," professing to believe the Bible but not knowing it or living it out. Your kids will spot your ignorance and hypocrisy a mile away. Instead, make the Bible's world your own world, and welcome your kids into that world.

Here are some key questions dealing with God, purpose, self-image, and spiritual strength that will serve as a checklist as your child matures.

Christian Worldview Checklist

Do your children understand that the universe is not a product of random, meaningless chance?

Have you explained to them why they are not just a cosmic accident, as our museums, zoos, TV shows, movies, and science textbooks are trying to convince them?

Do they know that the Bible stands up to the critics in its statements on science, history, and morality?

Have you made it clear to them that they were made in God's image, "crowned with glory and honor" (Hebrews 2:7; Psalm 8:5)?

Do they understand that it is their own sinfulness which has marred and ruined that beautiful image, and what the eternal and temporal consequences of that sin entail?

Do they grasp the fact that God is just when He judges?

Do they also understand the wonderful fact that sin has been dealt with? Have you told them exactly how it was dealt with, and that the crucified and risen Christ offers forgiveness for sin?

Do your children know that God offers to implant within them His own life, and His transforming power over sin?

Are they ever told how obedience to God is connected to freedom, love, and the entire biblical view of the universe?

Do they understand why God has made you as parents stewards of their character and safety, and why He and you are to be obeyed?

Have your children been taught that God loves them and offers them fulfillment through using them in exciting ways, if they will let Him?

Do they know that God has uniquely given *everyone*, including them—acne and all— individual traits and opportunities which He wants to use?

Do they grasp the fact that the Bible has prophesied a very concrete, realistic, and exhilarating plan for man's future?

The intellectual buttressing of such truth-claims will be the single most important factor in protecting them from such worldviews as secular humanism and its whirlpool of despair, or New Age teaching with its self-absorption.

I wish I could tell you to count on your church to imbed these truths into their souls. Sadly, I can't make that assumption. Instead, it's up to *you* to learn these facts and principles yourself, and become your child's discipler. You'll have no greater assignment in this earthly life, nor one more rewarding.

Reclaiming the Lost

For many parents, trouble has already begun, and the time for protection and preparation is long since past. Is there hope? Yes. The Bible is a book of *reclamation*, and its God is a God of redemption. In some way, all of us needed (and still need!) reclamation. You and I were reclaimed. Outstanding examples of biblical reclamations include Jacob (a habitual conniver), Matthew (a sleazy bureaucrat), and Paul (probably a murderer). As our heavenly Father disciplined and reclaimed these men, He also gives parents the hope, and even some of the tools, for reclaiming their children.

In every type of battle you'll read about, there are steps you can take and resources available to reach out to your child. I'm not saying it will be easy, or that success is guaranteed. But I'm convinced that as you turn these pages, learning about the battle, your eyes will be opened to factors you may never have seen before, and many of these can be a springboard to recovery. Often the beginning of the answer is seeing the problem clearly for the first time. In many cases, specific steps have been outlined, and my prayer is that as you take these steps, God will give you the joy known by parents all over America as their prodigal children come home.

CHAPTER THREE

Caution: Treachery at Work

Protection. Preparation. Reclamation. These are the gears that parents shift between in our world today.

There are two major areas where much of this shifting will take place: the powerful child-shaping realms of *education* and *entertainment*. In the last decade they have become the "deadly E's" of our youth.

Do you want to make your job of parenting a lot more easy? Then get a broad vision of how to shift the gears in these two areas. It will make the threats described in these pages much less intimidating and much more successfully managed.

Guerilla Training 101

In the following chapters you will learn things about the American educational system you might otherwise have thought unbelievable. You'll learn about suicide prevention courses that can cause suicide; about drug prevention classes that may increase the tendency to abuse drugs, and where the teachers are *prohibited* from saying that abuse is wrong. You'll encounter sex education programs which cause increased sexual activity, pregnancy, and abortion—perhaps by design.

Perhaps your child is sufficiently grounded in his faith to be able to chew up and spit out the humanistic coursework at the local elementary school. But if he's not, or if she hasn't made a Christian commitment, you'll need to do one of three things: Deprogram him each night, fight the course, or get your child exempted.

Don't send him into a den of wolves without training him to use the right weapons. Remember, toddlers should be kept out of the streets, and unprepared grade-schoolers out of the grasp of the skilled faith-crushers who design and implement such courses.

For that reason, before diving into such issues, you'll need to know that there are steps you can take to fight the system and protect and prepare your child. Here is an action plan you can apply to almost any situation you face in the public school system.

Watch, Pray, Act

Work on building a warm, secure, Christian home. Explain and reinforce a value system which will preempt meddling by educators programmed to tamper with your child's value system. Pray for your children, teachers, and school officials; pray specifically against the deception noted in this book.

Take an active interest in your children's schoolwork. Read their books. Talk with their teachers. Study to learn subtle techniques of values-changing and occultic programs, and the names of such programs. Be involved with the school system. The chapters of this book will help you pinpoint particular problems. However, there are some *general* things it will be helpful to know about up-front:

Detecting a problem. Is your child asked tricky ethical or moral questions about subjects which include life, death, religion, sex, or politics? Is your child at any time required or asked to voluntarily keep a journal or diary? Is he or she ever asked about your home life or lifestyle? Is religious commitment ever criticized? Have you noticed a change of behavior, especially with regard to attitudes about authority and right or wrong?

Kerby Anderson, vice president of Probe Ministries, warns parents, "If you suspect a problem... you need to get involved. If you are not sure, you need to ask more questions. I cannot think of a phone call I've received from a worried parent in the last few years that wasn't a legitimate concern. If you suspect there is a problem, then there probably is a problem and you need to get involved."[1]

Stepping in. This can be tough. Sally Reed, founder of the National Council for Better Education, once told me that both at teacher's college and when she was teaching in high school, her supervisors emphasized that it was best "to avoid a parent-teacher conference as much as possible." Here is the method prescribed:

> Challenge the parent on everything. I was told that if I never wanted this to happen again, I should make sure I made the parent as uncomfortable as possible. That is why so many parents go up to school only one time. They are made to feel like idiots, and never come back.[2]

Where was it happening? She said, "I don't know of a school district in America that is not doing this stuff."

But take heart! *Knowing* what you're facing opens the door for a successful strategy. If you suspect a problem, there are several concrete steps you can take:

1. Schedule an appointment with the teacher.
2. Ask to see the textbook and the curriculum, including the teacher's manual if necessary. Often this is

where the really incriminating material will be. You pay the taxes; it's your right. If the teacher refuses, then you're right to suspect a problem. Don't take no for an answer.

3. If the teacher says that the material is state-owned and can't be removed from the school, offer to take the materials to the library to examine them.

4. If you don't get cooperation, go directly to the principal, the superintendent, and the school board if necessary.

5. Copy or photocopy the material. Present it to the teacher, principal, superintendent, or school board.

6. Know your rights and exercise them. You can use the model "Hatch Amendment" letter (see the Appendix) to have your child excused from any classes you deem to be violating your parental rights. You may have to encourage your child to do so because he or she may feel like an oddball. But this is better than allowing a vulnerable child to be propagandized or manipulated in the way you'll discover in the pages to come.

7. Remember, the teacher is not necessarily your enemy. Often he or she is a pawn of powers far higher, who have a hidden agenda. So go in with an attitude of educating the teacher if you find a problem. If that doesn't work, however, then for the sake of your son or daughter it is time to get tough.

Network with Christian parents locally and across the country. Then, if you spot offensive material in your child's school, you'll be in a position to intervene at whatever level is necessary to solve the problem. If you meet resistance at the level of the school, use your network to intervene at the school-board level. Be bold. Such resistance is slowly reaping a harvest of success stories, as you will see throughout this book.

Guerilla Training 102

In the following chapters you'll also discover that whatever you thought about the entertainment industry's strategy for your child, the reality is probably worse. Areas of battle include all forms of behavior and many forms of belief, including suicide, sexual perversion, violence, the occult, and Satanism. This is especially so in the area of rock music.

Protection, of course, is necessary. This even extends into the teen years, and for social situations. Parties and playmates must be monitored according to your child's ability to cope with the temptations and deceptions that are roaming freely in today's adolescent interaction. Remember, this is not the 1940's or 1950's.

The main offenders will be music, movies, and TV. Sex, alcohol, violence, suicide, crass materialism, and the occult are common themes in children's entertainment and advertising today. As a good shepherd, you must train children to evaluate all media input through a Christian moral framework. But until the children can do this, entertainment must be screened and often withheld.

Yet what if protection and preparation fail? How do you reclaim your child from the trap of corrupting entertainment?

Prepare and Reclaim

Linda, a concerned mother from Alabama, called my show during an interview with Eric Holmberg, writer and host of *Hell's Bells*, the masterful video expose of rock 'n' roll (Reel to Real Ministries, Gainesville, Florida). Although the home environment was Christian, Linda's 14-year-old son was listening to Metallica, a group known for its promotion of despair, suicide, and Satanism. The signs of cultic devotion were all there: posters on the bedroom walls, as well as the group's name and symbol written all over school notebooks.

What should she do? Tear down the posters and ban the group? Eric replied, "That's a difficult age. If the child is mature [in his faith] and submitted to you, you can perhaps enforce a fiat. But if he's already rebellious, you must explain it to him and get him to see the evil for himself and think it through."

For objectionable music, the key to correcting the problem is to face the lyrics, which are the substance of the problem. This is a method of confrontation that has proven successful many times. Not only that, but its principles also apply to helping your child escape the grip of other forms of entertainment as well.

How does this method work? First, the parents must inform themselves. Second, they must confront their children. And third, they must maneuver their children into passing judgment on the words and messages of their rock heroes. The strategy is one of controlled confrontation of the evil, appealing to your child's innate conscience and, when appropriate, the Bible. Thomas Jipping, an expert on youth culture who works with troubled teens, outlines the strategy as follows:

> You have to face the issue directly with a young person. Kids know what the words are to these songs. They know what the lyrics and the messages are. Adults typically don't. Adults have to get to know what that message is, and then face it with that young person directly.
>
> Look at the lyrics directly. Talk about those lyrics—because the lyrics aren't mysterious and vague. Talk to that young person about whether deviant sex or suicide or murder and violence are good or whether that's harmful. Talk about it with them. Don't just say it's bad, shut it off, and do as I say. Face it directly.
>
> And then also talk about the many alternatives that are available today. Whether it's

Christian music or not, there is an unbelievable range of music today which does not
promote killing and hatred and sexual violence....Face the negative directly. Don't
sweep it under the rug. Face it directly. And
then offer the many, many positive alternatives in music that are available today.

Your child may need to be prepared to withstand the
moral perversion so prevalent today in music, on camera, or on the printed page. Or he may be already
involved, and need to be persuaded to walk away from it.
In either case, the evil simply must be exposed, and the
child must be forced to compare evil with good and then
make a conscious choice. Individual situations will
require different tactics, but the broad strategy will
seldom stray far from this course.

Above all, we must pray for our children constantly.
Beyond all we can do, only God can ultimately safeguard
our flock from the mounting dangers of our increasingly
corrupt culture. But because God commands shepherds to
be alert as well as prayerful, let's take our reconnaissance
of the battles with our eyes open and our swords drawn.

RESOURCES

Books:
> *Parent's Survival Guide to the Public Schools*, by
> Sally Reed

Video:
> *Hell's Bells*, Reel to Real Ministries, Gainseville,
> Florida

Organizations:
> National Council for Better Education, Alexandria,
> Virginia (Sally Reed, Founder)
> Citizens for Excellence in Education, Costa Mesa,
> California

CHAPTER FOUR

Competitive Parents, Healthy Children

By any measure, Jim and Pat were loving Christian parents. But now they were also very *distraught* parents, and their fears were mounting with each passing day.

The problem was Christie.

For 14 years she had been their darling. Raised in the church, she had shown true spiritual enthusiasm and in every way had been a very dedicated young Christian. Oh yes, there were the usual childhood problems, but nothing major—certainly nothing like *this*.

The signs of trouble began with the appearance of some new friends. They seemed a bit strange, but neither Jim nor Pat had wanted to say anything. After all, weren't people who didn't quite seem to fit in the very people Jesus mingled with in order to bring them to the light?

Pious reassurances crumbled, however, with Christie's radical change of personality.

A few polite questions were met with a defiant "It's *my* life, I'll live it how I please" attitude. Old friends were dropped as the new ones began monopolizing her time. It became clear that this was *not* just another phase.

Before long, rebellion was sprouting in every area of Christie's life—her dress, the way she talked, her refusal to obey, her new habit of staying out late. Especially disturbing was that she was now running around with a guy who obviously needed a long session at a barbershop.

By the time they went to see some old friends living in another state, Jim and Pat were literally beside themselves with worry and fear. After 14 years, were they about to lose their daughter to some unknown, unforeseen force?

The Unsung Heroes of the 90's

A crisis like the one Jim and Pat experienced has been repeated tens of thousands of times in homes across America in the last two decades.

In this chapter you'll meet five sets of adults, including Jim and Pat, with five different stories. It would be misleading to say these accounts are representative of *all* of the challenges parents face today. Neither are they blueprints for responding to the challenges *you* might be facing in raising your own children. There are simply too many types of situations, each with its own set of complications.

Nevertheless, these stories are real-life accounts of battle on the front lines of parenting in the 1990's. They show the guts and determination it takes to win—the strategic planning, the daring, the creativity, the ferocious tenacity of wrestling with a culture which often seems to have gone mad. But most of all, these are stories of victory—victory at home, victory in the schools, victory in the hearts and minds of children.

The Power of Truth

Sitting on their friends' living room sofa, Jim and Pat poured out their fear and grief concerning the "new person" who had seemed to replace their daughter.

Unexpectedly, their friends began asking about Christie's music.

"Well, we've always let her listen to just about anything she wanted," Pat replied. "We trusted her. And besides, other than being a bit hard on the ears, what can music do? Half the time you can't understand the lyrics of kid's music anyway, can you?"

Their friends' response was to give Jim and Pat a well-produced set of videos on the dangers of rock 'n' roll in the 1990's.

"I don't know if you're aware of it, Jim," said his friend, "but music has changed since we were kids. *A lot.* The music today openly advocates the worst kind of rebellion, violence, perverse sex, drug use, and more—even Satan worship and suicide. And studies show that the kids *do* listen to the lyrics and adopt their values.

"But at the same time, you can't just concentrate on the bad stuff," his friend cautioned. "You need to once again show Christie the light—the fallenness of man, the reality of spiritual evil, the Person of Christ, His death and resurrection, the power of the Holy Spirit, and the call to a holy life. You need to show her the darkness for what it is, show the light for what it is, hold them next to each other, and then pray that Christie makes the right choice. We'll be praying with you."

Jim and Pat left with much to think about. But they also left with some ammunition. And a little more than three weeks later they could hardly wait to call their friends.

"We looked at the videos," they said, "and of course we were shocked. But then we prayed, and made the decision that we needed to do more than just talk with

Christie—we needed to let her *see* the truth for herself. Frankly, we didn't know what would happen. At times we thought we might alienate her forever.

"But after she looked at those videos, and saw what was *behind* the music and the whole culture she had embraced, she came to us in absolute tears and brokenness. *It was a miracle!* We had a long, long talk about life—long overdue on our part. We had no idea what kind of world our Christian daughter had been tempted by.

"She said, 'I didn't realize what they were trying to do to me!' She made a total, 180-degree turnaround. She got rid of that sleazy boyfriend and changed the way she was living and her whole attitude—all as a result of seeing the truth. It's just amazing what a strategic dose of the truth can do in the hands of God. We have our daughter back, and now she's stronger than ever!"

A strategic dose of truth in the hands of God—that's often what it takes.

Yet if the parents don't know the truth, if they are totally ignorant of the plans the world has in store for their kids, how will those children ever be protected, prepared, or reclaimed? In Jim and Pat's case, they were able to quickly win back their daughter and prepare her for future tests.

But hopefully, not every parent will have to endure such a close call. What kinds of things are other parents doing to *prevent* such a nightmare from happening?[1]

"Our Children Are Not Lost!"

"I'm one of the baby-boomers," says Janet, a woman who called my talk show from Rhode Island one afternoon. "I'm in my forties. I have three teenagers, two in college and one in high school. I'm here to tell parents that it is possible to raise good, clean, chaste, drug-free teenagers. It takes an awful lot of work, but it is possible."

Janet is an example of a parent who has found a way to balance the two necessities of protection and preparation. She and her husband have also combined strong positive values in the home with a tough defense against outside threats.

She warns, "With everything we see in the headlines and in the news today, it's very easy to become discouraged and to think our children are lost. I want to tell parents, 'You hold on, and you hold on tight. They are not lost unless you give them up!'"

That's the message that needs to be heard: Our children are not lost unless we give them up. Indeed, this could become the battle cry for parents in the 90's. What are Janet's prescriptions for not giving up our children?

First, avoid the trap of passivity. "Christians parents have sat back and allowed our society to crumble into degradation and corruption unlike anything that's ever been seen before." The fight, in the opinion of this successful mother, must be fought on all fronts—education, entertainment, peers, even the political involvement by parents for the purpose of influencing the culture in which their kids will grow up.

Second, start the process of protection and preparation when your child is young. "Don't wait until they're teenagers to decide that this is not the music they should listen to or the TV they should watch," she says. "Even a very young child knows what's on TV and knows what's in the music. In any mall anyplace in the United States you'll find girls as young as four or five or six years of age who look and dress no different from their teenage sisters. But these are children; these are not mini-adults."

Third, take ownership of your child's development. For Janet and her husband this meant keeping the children close to the home, where they can learn the core values that will shape their lives.

She comments, "Don't fall for the lie that says a child *has* to go to preschool, *has* to go to nursery school, or else he won't be ready for kindergarten or first grade.... Most children can be kept at home until they are six or seven years of age. The home is where the child picks up all his values. He shouldn't be picking them up from a school that *has no values*, and from kids who are no better educated or better informed than he is."

Taking Control and Beating the Odds

A reactionary extreme, or a long-needed return to sanity? While it may not suit every family's circumstances, the home-based philosophy employed by this woman and her husband is picking up more support all around the country. The strategy can include options such as home schooling, sacrificing income to have a parent always at home, scheduling family times, and taking other measures designed to give children the deepest possible moral roots and the least amount of contamination.

It isn't luck when a parent like Janet can boast a successful record of rearing children into the teen years and beyond, especially in our culture. There's always a *method* behind the success. Ideas have consequences, and the right results are usually built by using the right methods based on the right foundations.

Janet and others of her persuasion are beating the odds in our society. They are busily raising intelligent, sensitive, and creative children whose lives are a legacy to the vigilant care of their parents. Janet reminds us that parents must be masters of the arts of protection and preparation. Children must not only be filled with the right values, but they must be protected against the invasion of the wrong values from the enemies found in every part of our culture.

Janet's exact approach might not be right for you, but the general priorities she articulates must be a part of the plan for every parent who wishes to be competitive in our culture.[2]

A New Tradition of Happiness

An expert on the home recently remarked that the traditional "nuclear" family is on the verge of a meltdown. Perhaps so. But it's also true that out of the ruins, new types of parents are rising up to build a new tradition of healthy and stable children.

One of these parents is Ray, from Gadsden, Alabama. "My wife and I both came out of broken homes; both our families were divorced," he recently said. "So we didn't have much of a background to grow on except what we started learning through Bible study."

In 1986 Ray, his wife, and their four children embarked on an action plan that he claims revolutionized their lives and cemented positive values in their children. The first step? They threw out the television.

Morally, TV is a 25-foot sewage line pouring its contents directly into your living room and your childrens' minds. Yet it is also a supreme device to numb the brain and destroy family solidarity. Viewed night after night, television disarms the ability to think critically and crowds out time that could be better spent building relationships among family members.

The radical course taken by Ray isn't what I would recommend for every family. For most, television viewing can be cut down to those features that will truly raise awareness of the important things in the world. Yet for some families, junking the TV is necessary to avoid the snares of temptation. According to Ray, the results have confirmed the wisdom of their cold-turkey approach.

"We have four children," he says. "We noticed over a time span of about a year that our kids' desires for all the latest things as far as toys and other paraphernalia had dropped off drastically, and they became more satisfied with what they had.

"At night," he says, "we actually *get together* as a family. We're kind of an oddity around here. We read *every* night. Mom usually reads a story to the boys and a lot of time the girls will listen. I have two girls who are thirteen and ten, and two boys who are four and almost two. There's conversation, and there's squabbling, but it's really a family atmosphere."

What would he say to other parents considering putting a clamp on the influence of media in their home?

"There are a lot of parents who feel like we do but are afraid to step out. It's real hard those first few weeks to do without the TV. It's hard to make yourself change your lifestyle, but with a lot of prayer *it can be done.*"

The most encouraging aspect of their lifestyle is the strength of their oldest daughter as she ventures into the teen years. He says, "We've tried to raise her in God's light, according to God's Word. We've been very up-front with her about how we fell down when we were younger, and why. Our oldest girl will pretty well stand up for what she knows is right and the values that we've taught her."

This kind of family management isn't a magic solution for every problem. Ray talks about how they are struggling with how to meet the challenge of their daughter's peers, most of whom come from an entirely different background. But at least for now, the course has been run without a mishap such as Jim and Pat encountered. In today's society, that's a gold medal performance with which any parent should be content.[3]

"You Can't Possibly Teach Your Daughter About Sex!"

In the area of peer pressure, perhaps Ray should talk to Leah. She and her husband learned that as children get older, supportive parents are often called upon to strengthen them to fight life's battles using the values they've been given during their formative years.

This hit home for Leah when she received a note from her daughter's public high school counselor that almost sent her through the roof.

Leah and her husband have four teenagers. They have made it a point to raise a warm, close-knit family. Along with attendance at an active church, the entire family listens to Christian radio—both issues-oriented and Bible teaching programs. They have even banded together with other such families for mutual support and the sharing of information and experiences.

"One of the things we found out," Leah says, "was that we could not trust the school system. We found this out over a period of time, and we refused to let our children participate in school activities involving sex education." In fact, Leah didn't think she could be surprised by *anything* the school system did. Not the condom demonstrations in class. Not the absence of instruction about condom failure rates and the danger of acquiring AIDS by practicing so-called "safe" sex. Not the implicit okay of "meaningful" premarital sex. Not even the tacit approval of "alternate" sexual lifestyles.

But then came the note. It was from one of her daughter's counselors, criticizing her and her husband for holding their daughter out of the sex ed classes. In part the note said, "You can't possibly teach your daughter about sex."

Leah was fuming. Who was this educrat to say that she, a mother of four, couldn't teach her own children about sex? Yet this was a tactic becoming routine for the public school system. The unspoken message was not that Leah couldn't teach her daughter about sex, but that she didn't have *the right* to do so, and was actually teaching her daughter things which contradicted the school's "broad-minded" position.

Of course, the counselor's fears were well-founded. A wholesome view of sex had been a part of her daughter's training all along. Yet Leah and her husband thought that if they quietly went about this training and then circumspectly withheld their children from sex ed, they could avoid making waves while giving their daughter the protection she needed. But when that note came crashing through the window of Leah's complacency, she and her daughter both knew they were in for a battle. Their strategy: counterattack.

The "Just Say No" Club

"Our daughter started a 'Just Say No' club at school that involves *abstinence* as an alternative to so-called safe sex," Leah explains. "A number of other girls have joined with her in this."

What do they do at their meetings? "The girls have set the standards for dating," Leah says, "and the standard is that you don't go out with any boy who intimates in any way that he's interested in you sexually. You watch your dating habits. You try to double-date or date at parent's homes...and you keep yourself out of dangerous situations."

The "Just Say No" club became a magnet for sensible advice and support for girls seeking direction on whether to become sexually active. The club meetings also carried presentations on AIDS, and began spreading the abstinence message to other girls in the school, many of whom were eagerly accepting it.

That's when the high school administrators decided this kind of rebellion had gone too far. With sexual purity threatening to become an epidemic, they moved to put a halt to the entire conspiracy. Leah's daughter was contacted and told that her club was throwing a wrench into the official program. They said, "We do not teach abstinence. That's not part of the curriculum."

But the young woman refused to back down. She responded, "But you tell us we can't smoke or take drugs. That's teaching abstinence."

Backed by their parents, and prepared with years of moral training, the girls stood their ground—and won. More importantly, they are winning the battle of life. They will not end up as another statistic in the rise of teen pregnancy or AIDS. They won't suffer the emotional scars of frivolous teenage sex. They will enter adulthood whole—light years ahead of most of their undisciplined, confused, and hurting classmates.

"We're really proud of the fact that our kids have taken a stand this way," says Leah. "We can complain about the schools and we can do through the system what we can, but it really comes back to the parents."

What's next for the "Just Say No" club? Their agenda is now expanding to include self-protection from manipulation in other areas of their schoolwork. When last heard from, the girls were circulating a fact sheet about New Age teaching in the classrooms.

Leah reports, "Even though the names of such courses change, the kids are now aware of the content and they say, 'I'm not going to participate in that.' And as parents, we have to give them the backbone to hold to their convictions."[4]

Wilderness Rescue

Sometimes parents are called upon to put their training to use when least expected, and for children other than their own. That was true for Donna.

When I talked with Donna, she had just been through one of the most horrifying, yet most rewarding, weeks of her life. A devout Christian woman, she had volunteered to be a counselor at a church camp near her home on the eastern shore of Maryland. The campers were 13- and 14-year-olds who were active in the youth groups of a conservative church.

As Donna and the other adult counselors began talking with the teenagers, they sensed the telltale marks of despair and rebellion. Because these adults knew the kind of environment that these and all other children must endure today, they started asking questions. What did they find? Most significantly, well over one-third of the 40 campers were involved in heavy metal rock music, Ouija boards, the occult game Dungeons & Dragons, and even seances.

Because Donna and the other counselors were aware of the high potential for self-destruction connected with these practices, they pressed further. They soon found that the teens were suffering from bouts of depression, much of it suicidal. In fact, the immediate area was a hotbed of occultic influence which had seen eight teen suicides in the past six months. The wolf was on the prowl. But this time the sheep were snatched from his hungry jaws. Alert shepherds had been on guard.

Here's the lesson: All it took to save the lives of a group of kids was a handful of concerned and knowledgeable adults (not professional counselors) who were ready to lovingly "poke their noses" into the crumbling world of these children. Once these adolescents saw the danger and were offered the concerned, down-to-earth help of a group of caring adults, the spell of death was broken and the road to victory was begun.

• • •

Competitive parents are the unsung heroes of the 90's, and they can be found in our neighborhoods wherever you look. I believe that with the right information, divine assistance, and your own willpower, that kind of parent can be found in *your* home as well.

Part
Two

BATTLES
OF BEHAVIOR

CHAPTER FIVE

America's New Barbarians

The character of our children is a leading indicator of our future as a culture.... When our children are sick of soul, there is no higher priority than to seek their healing.[1]
—Daniel Coats
United States Senate

Honor your father and your mother, that you may live long....
—Exodus 20:12

Isn't it strange how your children can be destroyed, your home ruined, and your future happiness erased by someone you may not even know exists? It's even more strange when that someone looks as harmless as Rachel Matthews.

During a recent summer, the 25-year-old Ms. Matthews was flying around the country in her position as a talent scout for Capitol Records. While sitting in an airport listening to demo tapes on her Walkman, she happened upon a musical group destined for the ears of America's youth.

The band's name? Rigor Mortis.

"It was just so intense and out of control," she later recalled, "just like caged psychosis going on. I loved it, because you could actually understand the lyrics. And even if they're morbid and gruesome, it's really cool that you could understand what they're saying. It makes it twice as evil. I like that."[2]

"Twice as evil" might be putting it mildly when referring to Rigor Mortis.

The tape that Rachel Matthews heard included songs such as "Die in Pain" and "Foaming at the Mouth." The band members get their inspiration from "gore movies," and even have their own private collection. Their video library contains titles like "Headless Eyes," "Evil Dead," and "Chopping Mall."

The lead singer once suffered a punctured lung when stabbed five times during a brawl. The guitarist sprained his foot while kicking someone in the face. Death and violence: They live it, they sing about it, they preach it as gospel. And for today's desensitized, emotionally damaged youth, it's becoming a religion more magnetic than any cult.

Why is it important for you to know about Rachel Matthews and Rigor Mortis? Let's look at two groups of children which our society is raising.

Barbarians at the Top

With fewer and fewer exceptions, American parents are raising "barbarians"—morally illiterate individuals who threaten to destroy their families, themselves, and our society.

What is a barbarian? In ancient history, the word usually denoted any external invader seeking to overthrow a prominent civilization. A modern definition, however, includes someone who attacks a society by openly shunning the values that make civilization both workable and worthwhile.

The first type of barbarians are the "upscale" brand— sophisticated individuals who specialize in everything from middle-class materialism, suburban restlessness, and corporate cruelty to shoddy ethics, white-collar crime, and the marketing of immorality. And all at a tidy personal profit. Bright, literate, well-educated, they occupy corporate and political positions of power in the society of tomorrow. Their only flaw: no moral anchor. In search of either the security blanket of materialism or the empty fulfillment of thrilling new experiences, they use their capabilities to seek their own selfish ends.

Rachel Matthews, climbing the career ladder in the music industry, is one of these barbarians. Talented and savvy, she can spot a promising artist from a song on an audition tape, yet at the same time turns a deaf ear to the havoc she wreaks through promoting the message of groups like Rigor Mortis.

Yet Rachel, who not many years ago was someone's little girl, is only one example. Upscale barbarians are all over the corporate world. One example is the crass materialist, epitomized so well by cynical inside trader Gordon Gekko, the character played by Michael Douglas in the movie *Wall Street*. Faced with an ethical dilemma, Gekko turns to his apprentice and reminds him, "It's all about bucks, kid. The rest is just conversation."

Despite Hollywood's often-pessimistic distortion of business people, there can be little doubt in the mind of anyone plugged into corporate or political life that real versions of Gordon Gekko are becoming more frequent. Sometimes they break the law, but more often the upscale barbarian is one of the millions of yuppies who live inside the legal boundaries of right and wrong while openly snubbing their Creator by worshiping at the altar of mammon. Indeed, the Reagan years brought a new force to American politics—the yuppie who loved Reagan for cutting his or her taxes and slicing regulations to increase profits, but who constantly railed at the administration for talking too much about moral issues like abortion.

The upscale barbarian has decided that religion is a formality at best, an obstacle at worst. He may even fool himself into adopting a religious veneer so he can sleep at night. This can be any kind of religion from born-again fundamentalism to kooky New Ageism. But his heart is narrowly focused on the here-and-now. Usually the upscale barbarian is a lover of either money, pleasure, or power. He could be an executive, a manager, a teacher, a skilled professional, a profitable technician, or a college or high school student. His ethics may be "clean" (getting caught breaking rules would be bad for the career) or "dirty" (anything goes except losing or getting caught).

The upscale barbarian is a tribute to the strength of the human mind that God created, because his or her material success shows that not every child can be intellectually and economically crippled by the educational system and the media. Yet he or she is also a testimony to the depravity of the human soul. Many of today's graduating youth have their moral and spiritual faculties completely gutted. Frighteningly, it is they who may largely dictate where our nation heads as we enter the coming century.

Barbarians at the Bottom

The second type of barbarian is the grass-roots guerilla. This type majors in activities such as street crime, family violence, and hatred or rebellion against parents, employers, and civil authorities. Ultimately he finds self-destruction. Many such barbarians are members of ghetto street gangs, but many others are not organized at all, and large numbers are raised in the soulless suburbs and smaller towns of America.

Robbed by our culture of career skills (as we will see in the next chapter) and given no moral limits, this type of individual tries to make up for his lack through lying, cheating, stealing, and even killing. He is supported by violence seen in video games and glorified in his entertainment and sports role models. One National Football League star said in a 1991 interview, "It's not good for business if you care for a second whether blood is bubbling from a guy's mouth."[3]

Many of the grass-roots barbarians spend time idolizing and imitating musicians like Rigor Mortis. Since being "discovered" by Rachel Matthews and signed to a contract with Capitol, Rigor Mortis has done quite well. They became a popular suburban band with a sizable cult following—one of hundreds of such groups across America. If your child can't happen to find a Rigor Mortis CD at a nearby record store or shopping mall, there is plenty of other mayhem and murder available from groups like Napalm Death, or in popular songs like "Breaking the Law" and "I Hate God."

To see the extremes to which such barbarianism can go, consider Rod Matthews. Fourteen-year-old Matthews was a suburban youth with a curiosity about death (as many kids have) and rental privileges from a neighborhood video store. The difference was that after viewing one too many slasher videos, Rod satisfied his curiosity by crushing the skull of a friend with a baseball bat. Immediately following his crime, he strolled to the home of another friend, and even took part in a snowball fight.

Was he conventionally insane? On drugs? Psychotic? Interestingly, a leading psychiatrist who studied the case said no. Instead, Rod Matthews was an example of a new but growing phenomenon. He was, in the psychiatrist's words, "morally handicapped."

Not every child in America will be a Rod Matthews, but the evidence is clear that many of them are walking at least partway down that path—sometimes a long way. In 1990 a prosecutor in Detroit stated that juvenile criminals "don't seem to give a hoot about human life." *The Washington Post* commented:

> While the severity of the actions ranges from simple cheating at school to pushing drugs to cold-blooded murder... the depth of the problem has reached a point where common decency can no longer be described as common. Somewhere, somehow... the traditional value system got disconnected for a disturbing number of America's next generation.[4]

The two types of barbarian, upscale and grass-roots, have different educational track records and follow different career paths, but under the surface they suffer from the same vital defect: a cracked moral foundation.

How to Fill an Empty Vessel

How does the cooing, adorable baby you brought home from the hospital grow up to be a teenager or adult who breaks your heart by defiantly spitting in the face of everything you value? How can he be headed off before he reaches "barbaric maturity," or helped once he has gotten there?

It is important to know that any modern barbarian is morally and spiritually empty. That truth holds a lesson for all parents. The major characteristic of the growing rebel is that other than self-interest, *he has no absolutes*—no moral straightedge anchored in anything above his own sinful thoughts and desires. How does this happen?

As with many things about human nature, it begins at the beginning. Babies are born totally dependent, totally self-centered, and totally demanding, if for no other reason than as a natural survival mechanism. But at some time the baby's will progresses to the point of rebellion. That's when parenting hits a critical juncture. Charles Colson aptly observes:

> Parents take small, self-centered monsters who spend much of their time screaming defiantly and hurling peas on the carpet and teach them to share, to wait their turn, to respect others' property. No other structure can replace the family. Without it, our children have no moral foundation. Without it, they become moral illiterates whose only law is self.[5]

From then on the parent must walk a tightrope by balancing heaps of unconditional love with mountains of swift and certain discipline—always making sure the child knows that both come from the same source. As the child grows, another essential ingredient added to the equation is the teaching of moral values and personal standards through example and explicit instruction.

What must your child learn in the family setting in order not to remain a "monster," first throwing peas, and later hateful words and fists? Here is a suggested order:

Love. Unconditional love should be present from the beginning. It supplies security and sets up critical lines of communication in later years. Researchers have identified this as a key factor in the first six to twelve months of life in producing future emotional health.

Rules. Discipline and standards must temper the child's sin nature when rebellion begins.

The Bible states that "rebellion is like the sin of divination [witchcraft], and arrogance like the evil of idolatry" (1 Samuel 15:23). The New Testament predicts:

> There will be terrible times in the last days.
> People will be lovers of themselves, lovers of
> money, boastful, proud, abusive, disobedient
> to their parents, ungrateful, unholy, without
> love, unforgiving, slanderous, without self-
> control, brutal, not lovers of the good, treach-
> erous, rash, conceited, lovers of pleasure rather
> than lovers of God (2 Timothy 3:1-4).

This biblical assessment describes today's barbarians, both upscale and grass-roots, with startling accuracy.

How then do we begin to civilize a child? One essential element is the assertion of parental authority through discipline. If done with the right attitude, it is the essence of love: "He who spares the rod hates his son, but he who loves him is careful to discipline him" (Proverbs 13:24). Yet discipline must be balanced with an open display of affection and sensitivity: "Fathers, do not exasperate your children; instead, bring them up in the training and instruction of the Lord" Ephesians 6:4).

God. Think about the last phrase of Ephesians 6:4, quoted in the previous sentence: "Bring them up in the training and instruction of the Lord." The Bible is telling you that your discipline must not come from yourself, but must come from God. This means two things: 1) Your punishment, instructions, and teaching of your son or daughter must be in line with God's Word; and 2) at the earliest possible age your children must understand that your authority over them is from God; they must see *why* the rules of your household are based on a biblical worldview.

One mother told her children, "I'm not telling you no to be mean. I'm doing it because I love you, and because

God loves you and has given me the job of looking after you."

I can almost hear you saying, "You mean our children must understand *why* the rules of the household are based on a biblical worldview? Doesn't that mean I have to know the biblical worldview myself, and figure out how it applies to my family? And then I have to somehow creatively convey this to kids who would rather watch cartoon videos than hear me say anything at all? It's impossible!"

This is an honest objection, but frankly, *you have no alternative.* The contemporary pull of barbarianism is so strong that backing off from the hard work of biblical parenting is like raising a white flag over your kids and letting the Devil come in and take them. If you're willing to work, willing to seek counsel, willing to labor at becoming wise, God will give you the resources to prevail. You *can* stand the heat, and you need to stay in the kitchen!

You may be making the false assumption that teaching your kids a biblical worldview and how it applies to practical rules of living is going to be boring to them. But if *you* get excited about the Bible and what it means for daily living, chances are that your kids can, too. See the "Christian Worldview Checklist" in Chapter 2.

What will he or she be learning? Things like the eternal value and dignity of every human being, and therefore the true vileness of lying, cheating, stealing, assaulting, and murdering. He will be learning the basis for human justice, and the certainty of divine justice even when human control breaks down. She will be getting a course in the authority of institutions such as the family, the church, and the government, all ordained by God to restrain evil. He will learn why service is the highest activity of man (and is a supreme imitation of Christ), as opposed to the current falsehood that "he who dies with the most toys wins." All of these principles flow from fundamental truths about God, man, the creation, and salvation.

One way or another, your children need to be fed a biblical worldview. Yes, "theology" must be the bedrock of practical living. Nothing else can be. Nothing else will work.

Once your child understands the biblical foundations for life and for your family rules, you are then set to apply more rules as the child grows. As you do, you will want to constantly explain to your son or daughter exactly why the rule or punishment is consistent with the worldview that has already been laid down as your family's foundation.

Your child must be allowed to see how love, rules, and God connect with each other. This is a real key to parenting success as the child grows older and encounters the forces that could seduce him or her into a life of rebellion.

Invaders at the Gate

Unfortunately, you'll get very little help from the world in your mission to raise a human being rather than a vandal. In his book *Against the Night*, Colson writes of the approaching sack of Rome by the barbarians of their day. The empire had become morally weak on the inside, and so the invaders found easy prey. But in our day the barbarians are vandalizing our culture from the inside.

Here are some areas of danger you need to be aware of, and some tips on how you can take added steps to protect your kids from joining the mob.

Rap music. We discussed conventional rock earlier in the chapter. But rap music, once a narrow black phenomenon, is now a broad cultural force with a heavy emphasis on rape, vengeance, assault, and murder, along with more conventional promiscuity. One expert estimates that *90 percent of young people in conservative churches* are involved in some degree of compromise regarding this form of music as well as excessive rock.

One of the top rap groups is the Ghetto Boys, who sing, "The sight of blood excites.../Shoot you in the head/ sit down/ and watch you bleed to death."[6] Why should we be surprised that our children are becoming enmeshed in a web of remorseless aggression?

If you haven't looked into the music your child is listening to, and sat down to initiate a loving but firm examination of why he shouldn't give it up if it fits this mold, I urge you to consider the words of writer Charles Krauthammer:

> As a psychiatrist, I used to see psychotic patients who, urged on by voices inside their heads, did crazy and terrible things. Now we have legions of kids walking around with the technological equivalent: 2 Live Crew wired by Walkman directly into their brains, proposing to "bust and break your backbone...I wanna see you bleed." Surprised that a whole generation is busting and breaking and bleeding? Culture has consequences.[7]

And what of the rap and rock that doesn't exalt crime and violence? Well, this type of music is for the upscale barbarian: Its themes focus on getting rich and getting pleasure, because little else exists in the world, according to rap.

Television, movies, and video games. The statistics speak for themselves. By age 18 the average child in our culture has seen 200,000 acts of violence on TV alone, and countless more on movie screens and rented videos.

What kind of violence did he see? Brutal killings and spectacular accidents with little of the lingering human consequences portrayed. People are rendered unconscious with a blow to the head, only to get up and "shake it off" seconds later.

Perhaps the most disturbing are surveys showing an increase in depictions of brutal assaults of attractive women. The assault scenes usually follow seconds after "cheesecake" footage designed to sexually arouse any male watching, thereby connecting in the mind of the viewer the feelings of sexuality and violence. It's a script for inducing rape or sexual perversion, and millions of young men are learning their roles all too well.

But the most personal source of violence may be video games, which lately have become schools of instruction in wanton death. The games are used personally and repetitively by kids in homes all over America. Some are harmless, but many are not. The games are highly personal to the user, but the deaths of the victims on the screen are highly *impersonal*.

How can parents cope, other than through the prudent measure of restricted viewing? The most straightforward approach is to simply sit down with your child and explode the mythology of media portrayals of violence. Point out the unseen consequences of violence left out of the story line on the shoot-em-up detective show or the ultraviolent Saturday morning cartoon, or even found in his favorite blood-and-guts comic or video game. Explain what happens to the brain when a person is knocked out. Use specific examples and appeal to his or her God-given conscience.

While joining with other Christian groups to curtail such violence in the public realm, be sure to wage your own campaign within the four walls of your home.

Hole in the Moral Ozone

I was recently told of a boy in a typical family who began to undergo mysterious changes in behavior. For

years he apparently had been an average likable youngster—the usual problems, but nothing especially dire.

But when he entered the second grade, troubling
episodes of rebellion began. Finally, when asked by his
parents one day to retire to his room to do his homework,
he dropped his books, put both hands over his ears, and
shouted, "I have my rights!"

After investigation, the parents found the problem:
"Values clarification" curricula in the boy's school,
exposing him to concepts such as the absence of any
right or wrong, and the right of every person, at whatever age, to determine what's best for himself. On top of
that, his class participated in pseudotherapeutic exercises designed to help him "get in touch" with his "real"
inner feelings. And since all humans are rebels under
the skin, rebellion is what popped out.[8]

Christina Hoff Sommers, a professor at Clark University, relates a chilling episode of this kind of "values-
free" education. It illustrates why, under the domination of this philosophy for the past two decades, our
schools are producing what ethicist Michael Josephson
has termed "a hole in the moral ozone layer" of our
nation.

A young teacher, fresh from workshops on values-
free instruction, conducted an approved exercise in
which the students were asked, "How do you feel about
homemade birthday presents? Do you like wall-to-wall
carpeting?" and so on. Then, in the middle of the series
of such questions and answers, she asked, "How do you
feel about abortion?" and "What do you think of hit-
and-run drivers?" The reaction to these questions was
elicited from each student in the same tone of voice, as if
one's *personal* preference in *all* instances, both mundane
and jarring, was all that mattered.[9]

Then came the day when her sixth-graders, after
being well-schooled in this system, announced that they
personally valued cheating on tests! Stuck for a good

comeback, the instructor eventually told them she was *personally* against cheating, and since it was *her* class, cheating would still be penalized. This sincere but badly misguided teacher then said, "In my class you must be honest, for I value honesty. In other areas of your life you may be free to cheat."[10]

It is hardly surprising then, that we get responses like these from college students today:

- A majority of students in a class at Harvard don't believe that anyone was really to blame for the Holocaust.

- Students in an ethics class concluded, "Torture, starvation and humiliation may be bad for you or me, but who are we to say they are bad for someone else?"

- Evaluation forms reveal, "I learned [in school] there was no such thing as right or wrong, just good and bad arguments."[11]

Your at-home moral education for your children gains strategic direction when you understand the type of persuasion your children are facing from the outside. They need your instruction. They need to have good role models pointed out to them. They depend on *you* to help screen their world for moral agnosticism and to help them face its seductive appeal.

Why Johnny Can't Succeed

A sluggard does not plow in season, so at harvest time he looks but finds nothing.
—Proverbs 20:4

Do you see a man skilled in his work? He will serve before kings...
—Proverbs 22:29

Every parent dreams of saying with pride, "My child the _____."

This is not just an improper "worldly" impulse. Career and money are frequent biblical topics. The book of Proverbs and the New Testament are filled with directives for successful and fulfilling work. Money is mentioned hundreds of times in the Bible.

Yet the dreams of parents are being shattered today by an epidemic of ignorance, laziness, and greed infecting their children. It is destroying not only children, but the future freedom and prosperity of the United States.

Businesses struggle to cope with millions of incompetents produced by our schools, and other nations snicker as our economy sinks. Our children, out to make a fast buck with few qualifications, see their standard of living drop and the population of street people inevitably rise.

Ignorance and laziness: the twin terrors of the 1990's. But just as the causes of these cancers are the same, their cures are also closely linked. They have to do with the way we teach our children in school, and the way we raise them at home.

Profile of a Prosperous Child

In terms of knowledge, skills, and occupation, what kind of child should you want? What sort of child will bring you the honor the Bible says that every parent should crave? According to the Scriptures, every parent should be proud of a son or daughter who—

- is using the mind God gave him to explore and enjoy His creation (Genesis 1:28; 2:19).

- has a strong moral compass (Proverbs 12:26).

- finds a calling in life consistent with his or her competence and desires, including homemaking (1 Thessalonians 4:11; Proverbs 22:29; 31:10-31).

- is content whatever the material circumstances, desiring to be neither rich nor poor, yet able to handle either (Philippians 4:11-13; Proverbs 30:8).

- knows the value of wise planning (Proverbs 21:5).

- knows how to manage finances (Proverbs 22:3; 28:19).

- is generous to the poor (Proverbs 28:27; James 2:2-17).

- gives to God and His work (Philippians 4:15-17).
- is dedicated to family and committed to providing for their material needs (1 Timothy 5:8).
- can pass on an inheritance to children and grandchildren (Proverbs 13:22).

Raising a child like this will be more difficult for you than it was for your parents or grandparents. At the head of your list of roadblocks is an educational system which is succeeding at its self-defined goal of "socializing" your child at the expense of educating him.

Education Takes the Plunge

What are the main causes of ignorance in America? One of the largest is a public educational system which has *deliberately* abandoned the quest for teaching hard, rational thinking.

Let's briefly go back to the beginning of our nation. In those days Christianity fashioned American culture, and especially American education. What kind of people did it make us?

The Christian God of the colonists was a *rational* Being. He had created a universe of regular laws. He had created man in His image to *rationally* explore the absolute truths of this brilliantly ordered environment. Building upon these assumptions, Christian parents vigorously educated their children, emphasizing literacy and the study of nature as a means of glorifying God. Educational techniques began with rote learning of math and spelling, and mastering the all-important rules of communication by which God has allowed mankind to construct civilization and escape the jungle.

Even with no public education, literacy rates were extremely high and the general populace well-educated.

Most people are astonished to learn that *born-again Christians* founded colleges such as Harvard (1636) and Yale (1701) for the training of ministers and Christian scholars.

But in the mid-1800's a plunge began. What went wrong?

It started when the Christian culture sagged under a bombardment of atheism, mysticism, and heresy from Europe in the late 1700's and early 1800's. The Christian leadership of Harvard was overthrown in 1805 by Unitarians and liberal Christians. That same period saw the growth of the public school movement, starting with the work of anti-Christian socialists such as William Channing.

Under the blitzkrieg of Darwin's evolutionary theory in the last half of the century, Bible-based Christianity was thrown into confusion and retreat in America. Liberal Christianity became a virtual arm of secularism, and fundamentalists began their disastrous pullback into smug isolation and cultural irrelevance. Into this vulnerable mess rode John Dewey, founder of the Teachers College of Columbia University, in the early 1900's.

The Flameout of Secular Education

Dewey fit the mold of other atheistic social engineers of his time such as Vladimir Lenin in Russia (with whom he agreed about the ideal organization of society) and Margaret Sanger in the United States (the racist founder of Planned Parenthood). His influence on modern education is unrivaled. Dewey's core tenets were that—

> there is no God and there is no soul. Hence ... immutable truth is also dead and buried. There is no room for fixed, natural law or moral absolutes.[1]

Sally Reed, president of the National Council for Better Education, points out that Dewey aimed public education toward the goal of shaping social values. He cared little about sharpening the abilities of the individual to discover natural and moral truths, concepts for which Dewey had no room in the first place. In fact, Dewey confessed the need for *less* literacy when he wrote:

> It is one of the great mistakes of education to make reading and writing constitute the bulk of school work the first two years.... It is not claimed that by [my] method suggested, the child will learn to read as much, nor perhaps as readily in a given period as by the usual method....[2]

One of Dewey's more prominent disciples even *praised illiteracy* as a vehicle to make children less apt to eyestrain and more open to social change!

As a result of this devaluation of hard-skills learning, American educational designers embarked on a journey of experimental methods for conveying knowledge to children. All of these new methods downplayed techniques such as rote memorization of math and phonetic (sounded-out) reading. Phonics depended too much on those silly rules of language! Instead, the Deweyites emphasized methods which focused more on inner impressions, group interaction, and visual stimulation, and less on the crucial ability to digest facts, formulas, and rules.

At the same time, history lessons began to dwell less on dates and events, and more on broad themes and subjective interpretation—and, as we shall see in a later chapter, on blatant propaganda. Geography became a game; children were taught to *make* maps, not read them. Usually they did neither very well. Anything

which riveted little Johnny's mind on hard, objective
truths and standards was discouraged.

That was about the time little Johnny began to get
poor national test scores. But then, competitive standards and rigorous testing were also discouraged by the
Deweyites.

The Case of the Missing Facts

Just how bad can it get? Ask Jane Nelson, a member
of the Texas Board of Education. In 1991 Mrs. Nelson
was shocked to find that *several hundred* factual errors
were present in history texts from a nationwide publisher, ready to go into Texas schools.

Her press conference startled and angered parents
all over the country, since the books were destined for
schools outside of Texas and across the nation. Errors
were gross and plentiful. The books stated that Truman
had dropped the atomic bomb on Korea, not Japan. That
Lyndon Johnson was still president in 1972, even though
he had retired in 1969. That the slaves were freed in
1963—off by only 100 years! Many observers joked that
the books could only have been authored by someone
educated in the American public school system!

The textbook company pledged to correct the errors
and resubmit the books. But when they brought them
back in 1992, guess what? Most of the errors still
remained!

That's when the plot began to thicken. It became
clear that the educational bureaucrats and their cohorts,
the textbook publishers, viewed the teaching of factual
accuracy not as a front-burner issue but as a nuisance to
be swept under the rug. When Mrs. Nelson demanded
that the books be rejected once again, she was attacked
by the chairman of the education board as an extremist,
and debate on the substance of the issue was abruptly
cut off.

As for the publisher of the textbooks, Holt-Rhinehart, its official summation of the matter was this: "There is more to teaching U.S. history than the teaching of dates." Unanswered went the question, *What "more" can there be* when hundreds of foundational dates and facts are totally wrong? Only in a Deweyian system could such an outrage have occurred in the first place, and then have been allowed to continue by educators seemingly unable to fathom the problem!

As a final blow, the board voted to prohibit any private citizen, such as the well-known researchers who found the errors (Mel and Norma Gabler), from engaging in future exploration to find textbook errors. It was a classic case of "Don't bother me with the facts." Sadly, the children reading the textbooks won't be enriched by the facts, either.

Teaching Johnny Not to Think

If the course designers of today's schools aren't spending time teaching children the basics, what *are* they doing? Again, it goes back to the attack on children's ability to rationally think. That attack has come in two waves.

The first wave was led by Dewey and his followers, and there is no question that it still continues. They not only had a bagful of techniques which eroded our children's basic skills and withheld from them crucial facts and figures, but they also cut the hours spent on skills and fact-finding, and instead dedicated precious classroom time to pursuits such as—

- Disguised psychotherapy
- Political indoctrination
- Values modification.

These and other programs were based on the educational elite's conviction that, as one prominent Harvard professor told a packed convention of teachers, children are "mentally ill" if they have been raised by parents who hold traditional family and moral values. And it followed Dewey's original premise that the key to education was reprogramming such values, not developing skills and discerning truth.

But there has also been a second great wave, one which is still gathering strength today. This is the invasion of the New Age movement, another form of humanism that builds upon the foundation laid by secular humanists but uses New Age weapons which John Dewey could scarcely have imagined.

Education by Hypnosis

The most damaging New Age idea for our children is a madly escalated attack on objective truth and rational thinking. The New Age theorists who designed the public school courses which pervade the system today believe that 1) physical existence is an illusion, 2) we can mentally tap into forces that change physical reality, and 3) we are all perfect expressions of godhood. Using methods that are sometimes subtle, sometimes blatant, these religious zealots have planted their doctrines into virtually every school district in America.

One result of this is mysticism. An alarming number of students are taught classic Hindu and occultic meditation (often labeled as "relaxation" training). Meditation—the obsession with looking *inward*, bypassing rational thought, and escaping reality—is practiced to the tragic neglect of developing skills for the real world that God created for us to live in. Meditation may sometimes have temporary benefits (one teacher told me, "It does calm the children down"), but the long-range patterns have proven to be disastrous to intellect, drive, and career. To get an idea of where we're headed, just think of the dismal gross national product of India, the mystic meditation center of the world outside of the American classroom.

An offshoot of mysticism is self-centeredness. The reasoning is that since I am divine, I decide what's right or wrong for me. Inner feelings become life's primary guidelines rather than a healthy, honest observation of reality. The catchphrase of the youth of our day is "If it feels right, just do it."

Because of this total focus on inner thought, a healthy "self-esteem" has become the obsession of counselors, curricula, teachers, and students. This preoccupation tends to produce children who are either very arrogant or very depressed. Usually they are diverted from acquiring the knowledge and skills that once oriented children to reality, led them to their role in God's creation, and helped provide that psychological security which is so elusive today.

The more money that is pumped into self-esteem training in schools, the higher the drug and suicide rates climb. Is this coincidence? All too many of these students are deprived of true learning by being told to look inside for their own divinity but finding, as the Bible predicts, nothing there.

The Case of the Mangled Letters

Another result of the second wave of modern education is what is called relativism. Students believe there is no right or wrong way to live, work, or think. This is another formula for dropping out of life and abandoning the discipline necessary to contribute to society and attain personal fulfillment. It is also a pathway to programmed illiteracy.

The following true story at first made me laugh—until I started hearing similar accounts from parents in various parts of the country.

A woman from Jefferson City, Missouri, called my talk-show to complain about her son's teacher wasting class time. Instead of spending more hours teaching math and grammar, this instructor was encouraging the children to spill their guts about private matters to a fuzzy doll handed out on the first day of school. This was in the second grade, and boys were included. This is a typical bit of educational psycho-nonsense, and this part of her story didn't surprise me.

What *did* catch me off guard was this distraught mother's remark that the children were deliberately encouraged to *misspell* words on assignments.

"Allowed to misspell words?" I replied with a chuckle. "I wish they would have had that when I was in school!"

But she persisted. "It's called 'Inventive Spelling,' with a note to parents telling them not to be alarmed if spelling assignments are brought home wrong."

As it turns out, programs like this one are springing up all over the country. It's another scheme to stimulate little Johnny's creativity and self-esteem, and enhance his "decision-making" capacity. As with all values clarification courses, right or wrong answers aren't the point; the important thing is that the child learns that *he* calls the shots, that *he* is in total control.

Control with no ability to communicate? To discern truth from error? To relate to fixed standards outside his own private world? Like absence of social manners, this intellectual rudeness will lead only to mental and cultural chaos, and turn our children into beggars.

Has Your Home Become a Welfare State?

Having read this far, you probably recognize that the "dumbing down" of our children isn't just a product of the schools; it is also supported by other enemies pouring into your home. And your home is where the counterassault must begin.

These enemies are dangerous for two reasons. One is the message. Similar to the secular and New Age humanism in schools, the "if it feels right, do it" message preached by TV, movies, music, and magazines attacks tough-minded thinking and promotes undirected laziness. Yet there is also a second danger. Not only is the message of the media deadly to intelligence, drive, and career, but it is the medium itself—the method of conveying the message—that kills. This is true even when something neutral or positive is being communicated. The truth is that our media-addicted children are turning into empty-headed couch potatoes and other varieties of mental vegetables. If you doubt this, consider these facts:

> Preschoolers are spending more time watching TV than it will take them to earn a college degree.

> By the time the American child has completed high school, he will have spent 22,000 hours of TV—twice the amount spent in classrooms.

> Adults, the role models, spend 40 percent of their leisure time watching TV, putting it only behind sleep and work as time spent doing any activity.

One observer recently wrote, "The real evils of the entertainment industry are not the violence and profanity—offensive though they are. It's the banality: the sheer waste of time. When we turn the TV on, we turn our minds off; studies have shown that the analytical areas of the brain nearly shut down during extended TV viewing."[3]

Compounding the problem is the fact that our children today seem to think that money grows on trees. Yet why shouldn't they?

Think about the pattern of the last three generations. During the depression of the 1930's, many children had to work hard to help their families eat more than one meal a day. When those children had their own families in a more prosperous time, they pledged "never to let that happen to my kid." So they gave them everything they never had while growing up, and they spoiled them. They gave them pleasure and a good education, but robbed them of the precious example of a family who could pull together to cope with hard economic reality.

Today it is the grandchildren who are suffering. Modern parents tried to repeat the pattern of the 50's and 60's. Kids are still being pampered at home, yet now their education is poor and the long-range economy may be tightening like a noose. That's four strikes against them: a poor education, media addiction, no home discipline or responsibility, and a sagging economy. The sum of that equation is going to be the streets, welfare, or lifelong frustration—unless you step in now.

Solving Your Educational Crisis

Whether or not our country can solve its collective educational crisis, *you* can do much to protect or redeem your child's mind and career. But it begins with your attitude. It's time to take responsibility for your child's education, because the government clearly can't manage it.

Does this mean home schooling? Perhaps, but not necessarily. There are many alternatives to the path of total public education for your child. The one you choose will be an outgrowth of your personal circumstances. But clearly, one or more of them *must* be chosen, because depending totally on state schools could be suicidal for your child's future.

If you elect to keep your child in public schools, you'll certainly need to supplement your child's education with home learning. Your goals are to compensate for any miseducation by deprogramming your child of bad learning techniques and habits, and to replace them with solid learning. This will take a commitment on your part—perhaps as much as an hour or two per night. You will look over your child's homework, do it with him, and supplement it with your own lessons. And before that, you'll need to do research to bring yourself up to speed on how to accomplish this kind of educating.

You'll need to know how to teach phonics to your child. Once you see the incredible improvement and know that your son or daughter is leaping ahead of others, this won't seem like such a chore at all! You will need to know how to teach them math using "the old-fashioned methods"—the ones that work! Again, the happy results will spur you on. And above all, you will need to read to your children early and often. Read them the classics. Train them to love literature, not mind-numbing TV.

Will it be easy? No. Can it be done? Most certainly. But if you care about your child, it *must* be done. The school situation in America is too bad to let the secular educators have your child all to themselves.

Fortunately, resources and organizations are springing up to help you, as parents all over the nation are faced with the same problem and are learning to handle it superbly. My first recommendation would be to contact the National Council for Better Education (Washington D.C.), and Citizens for Excellence in Education (Costa Mesa, CA). Both are listed in the Further Help section of this book.

Two other alternatives exist: private schools and home schooling. These are enormous subjects requiring

considerable research on your part to see if your family
is right for either one. If you're contemplating Christian
schools, check them out very carefully on several bases:
adherence to doctrine, quality of education, accredita-
tion, financial stability, and board members. Regarding
home schooling, the absolute essential is to plug into a
strong local network of successful home school families
and learn from them. There are 300,000 home schools in
America today, compared with only 12,000 two decades
ago. Examine the different curricula and methods carefully. One man told me, "Home schooling isn't an
activity, it's a lifestyle; it's not something you *do*, it's
something you *are*."

The sacrifices are great, but the rewards are high.
I've had callers repeatedly tell me about miraculous
changes in their children's behavior, learning, and attitude when removed from public school, and tragic
declines in these areas when children go from a private
or home educational setting into the government schools.
Test scores for children of good Christian schools and
home schools consistently beat the national averages. If
you're up to it, these alternatives demand to be strongly
considered.

Home As a Launching Pad

Social commentators have described the modern
American home as merely a hotel for a loosely connected
group of busy and harried people. Don't let this happen
to you. If it already has, put an end to it.

The first step is to make *people* a priority in your
schedule. Make it a rule to have a certain minimum
number of meals together, with no TV or reading.

In fact, resolve to make the media, especially TV, an
advantage instead of a time-waster. Outline what kinds
of shows will be watched during restricted TV hours.
Attack the growth of mental mildew by watching only

good TV, which in these times may add up to very little. And as I mentioned earlier, read *in front of* your children, *to* your children, and *with* your children.

The other key piece of your strategy is to cultivate financial responsibility in your kids from an early age. The first step is to begin with the Bible. Many excellent books are on the market spelling out the financial principles found there, and you'll be amazed at the Bible's powerful practical financial advice.

Then construct a family budget by first tracking your cash flow. *The key here is to let your kids participate in the process.* Let them see your model of responsibility, and bring them into that pattern of life. Teach them about finances early, so that money management becomes both a skill and a habit.

Next, start a family "Job Corps." Teach your children the value, satisfaction, and rewards of work by giving them family jobs which they *must* do as part of the team. Then give them extra jobs for which they are paid. It may be a little hard for them when they're young, but it will become an ingrained ethic by the time it counts most—when they have a family of their own.

Also, teach your child the value of money. Let children in on important financial discussions and decisions. Teach them principles of saving, investing, earning, insurance, and more.

What if your child is older and already set in a negative pattern? First, as much as possible, take the above steps anyway, since they can only help. Second, be willing to invest your money, if necessary, in a good college-level (or private) course in finances for your child. Go with him or her if necessary.

The old saying is true, "If you give a man a fish, you have fed him for a day. If you teach him *how* to fish, you have fed him for a lifetime." You need to begin teaching your kids how to fish—before the lake freezes over.

RESOURCES

Books:

Minding Your Own Business, by Raymond and Dorothy Moore (on home-based family business and teaching children responsibility)

Working at Home, by Lindsey O'Connor

Home by Choice: The Effects of Mother's Absence, by Brenda Hunter, Ph. D.

The Stay-At-Home Mom, by Donna Otto

CHAPTER SEVEN

The Trap of "Safe Sex"

Rock 'n' roll is about sex. And I'm here to corrupt the youth of America.
— Rock superstar
Elvis Costello

It is God's will that you should be sanctified: that you should avoid sexual immorality.
— 1 Thessalonians 4:3

The night was September 25, 1991. A very important night in the life of Doogie Howser, M.D.

Just who is Doogie Howser? Why, he's one of the most important people in the lives of hundreds of thousands of pajama-clad, preteen kids who watch him religiously each Wednesday just before jumping into bed.

In his half-hour TV show, child prodigy Doogie, a fresh-faced kid with red hair and dimples, is an 18-year-old doctor. He has grown up before the eyes of America

ever since the enormously popular program began airing on ABC in the fall of 1989. Yet the 1991 season
premiere found Doogie with a problem that his medical
training just couldn't solve. In his words, "Being a vir-
gin is driving me nuts!"[1]

And so, on that fateful September evening, Doogie
and his girlfriend Wanda did something about it. They
did it at about 9:20 P.M., Eastern and Pacific time zones
(8:20 P.M. Central). Predictably, the ratings went through
the roof. I certainly wish more parents and advertisers
would have, too.

Driving with License

Aren't the producers of Doogie Howser, M.D., whose
main target audience is preteen and teenage children,
aware of the skyrocketing pregnancy rates of unmarried
teens? Are they ignorant of the fact that AIDS and a
slew of other sexually transmitted diseases are spreading through this age group faster than any other? Don't
they realize that seeing one of their role models "having
at it" is going to encourage replication of that behavior
in children already desensitized and on the brink? Or
that it will further stigmatize those who haven't compromised?

The obvious answer is that the producers of this
show are neither ignorant nor unaware. Instead, they
are representative of a culture which has been hijacked
by sexually liberal elites and has detoured away from
the values that once supplied the moral fiber our society
needed in order to function. These elites have seized
control in two major areas. The first area is entertainment, including television, rock music, music videos,
movies, and even certain comic books. The second area
is the entire sex education and "family planning" industry, including school sex educators, abortionists, sex-
ologists, and many psychologists. Of course, many politicians are busy running interference for both.

With these groups at the wheel, our society is careening toward sexual anarchy and moral destruction. And unless you are alert enough to step in, the victims will include your children.

In the 50's and early 60's our nation flirted with sexual taboo. We were kissing in the shadows, but usually we came home by midnight. In the late 60's we lost our virginity. Somewhere in the 70's we woke up to find we were prostitutes. But by then it was too late, especially for the offspring we had produced.

On the average day in America, 7700 teens relinquish their virginity. Most of these are unmarried, and many are younger than 15; 2800 teens get pregnant, and 1100 have abortions. In one middle-class, suburban school in Colorado, 26 percent of eighth-graders and 42 percent of tenth-graders admitted to having had sex at least once.[2]

Are evangelical kids exempt? According to author and youth expert Josh McDowell, one survey of 500 church youth yielded 62 percent who anonymously admitted they had been involved in *oral* sex. He estimates that six of every ten evangelical church youth are now involved in sexual activity.

At the same time, the greatest increase in AIDS cases is in those in their twenties, meaning that many young people contracted it in their teens.[3] Yet teens seem blind to this danger as promiscuity continues to surge and schoolhouse lessons on "safe" sex seem to backfire, merely heightening the teenagers' passions.

America's New Idol—"Meaningful" Sex

"All we tried to do was be honest," said Doogie Howser executive producer Vic Rauseo. "He's been in love with this girl for two years. And it seemed it would be dishonest, it would make him kind of weird if nothing happened."[4]

The relationship, you see, was "meaningful." That's a word that unlocks all the doors today. "Meaningful-ness" is being used to justify sex with any man, woman, child, animal, or thing, depending on who you talk to and what state of mind they're in when you talk to them.

"We have researched many organizations," says Linda Morris, Doogie Howser's other executive producer, "and most of the statistics show that teenagers are having sex. And that at the age of 18, approximately three-quarters of all teenage boys have had sexual relations. So I don't think we're breaking any new ground here."[5] Not breaking new ground? That's where she is tragically wrong. The "new ground" that is being broken is the direct TV marketing assault on your child's mind, using sensuality as a Rototiller.

This was displayed in all its brute force in a *TV Guide* interview with the young star of another hit show directed at children, Beverly Hills 90210, produced by Fox. In the interview, actress Shannen Doherty revealed her behind-the-scenes battle with the program's writers and producers to keep the integrity of the character she plays in the show.

Shannen's role is 15-year-old Brenda Walsh, a highly principled Midwestern girl thrown into the pressure cooker of a Southern California high school. The show's popularity has led to girls all over America imitating Brenda Walsh's hairstyle and writing Doherty letters asking for advice. Brenda Walsh is now an American teen role model.

At one point she battled the writers who wanted the already-thin Brenda to start worrying about her weight. Doherty said, "I sat down with Chuck Rosin [an executive producer] and said, 'Chuck, I'm the thinnest girl on the show! If girls hear Brenda say she can't go to the beach unless she loses weight, they're going to become anorexic! So many girls already have this problem.'"

She fought a good fight and won her case. The script was changed.

But the producers weren't finished; they had something more interesting in mind. You see, Brenda was going to give in to her pressuring boyfriend. And she would enjoy it—a necessary rite of passage. Doherty resisted again, but this time to no avail. The producers managed to force their will over the script, and in doing so psychologically raped an audience of young female fans.[6] *This is the new ground that is being broken.*

Hollywood's Sexual Agenda for Your Children

As media analyst Dr. Robert Lichter has noted, "Portrayal of sex on television has increased dramatically over the past fifteen years, and the rise in sexual themes and explicitness shows no sign of abating."[7] The reasons for this are threefold.

First, sex sells. The bottom line is the bottom line. And today, the children's market represents one of the most lucrative bottom lines available.

Second, surveys of television executives confirm that the vast majority actively endorse the free sex mentality, seeing little wrong with "meaningful" premarital, extramarital, and homosexual relationships.

Third, television aimed at children is becoming a tool of the "family planning" industry, which sprang from the sexual revolution of the 60's and is busily carrying forward its agenda behind the mask of respectability. Serving as consultant for Beverly Hills 90210 was the Center for Population Options, which favors liberal sex industry social policy such as school-based health clinics, abortion, and the largely ineffective "safe sex" education in schools.

But now a new trend is clearly emerging. During the fall '91 season, four prime-time programs aimed for kids featured loss of virginity as the theme. Instead of sexual license aimed primarily for the adult viewing audience, it is being targeted for children and portrayed in a highly favorable manner. The message is clear: Don't be "weird." Don't be driven nuts by the scourge of abstinence until marriage. Just find someone "meaningful" and do it. It's a trend we haven't seen before in that most powerful of all behavior-influencing media, television. But if instances like the fall '91 season go unchallenged, you can expect to see more.

Adult Movies...Made for Your Child

The assault on your children's hormonal glands is not unique to the television tube. Movie manipulators learned long ago that if sex sells, it sells especially well to children. They also learned that if a person's preferences are established by sexual input during childhood, he or she will keep coming back for more when older. The media sexperts know that once they program your child's psychological buttons, they can keep pushing them again and again.

Yet even this won't satisfy the appetites of today's entertainment moguls. Each year the sleaze threshold seems to be worse than the year before. Movies are going farther than ever to exploit your children, and at a younger age. NC-17 movies are a good example. This new rating category is a blatant ploy to get raunchy, X-rated movies out of the skid row adult theater and into the neighborhood movie house. Sexually graphic, otherwise X-rated films that are deemed to have true "artistic merit" will be given this rating, making them available for wider distribution, younger viewers, and expanded advertising. But how does the artistic elite define "art"? If the graphic homoerotic and pedophilic photographs by the perverted Robert Mappelthorpe can hang in major galleries around the country, funded by tax dollars, then what kind of "artistic" films will be showing at the mall cinema under the guise of NC-17?

Trouble also waits on the more "mild" side of the ratings spectrum, where the typical XXX-rated plot is simply geared down a couple of notches, with cheap innuendo substituted for explicit nudity. Yet the seductive appeal will be the same, and the psychological conditioning of your child's mind will be only slightly less intense. What he sees will help set his model for sexual fulfillment for years to come.

Music: Wolves in Not Much Clothing

If your children are decent enough to steer clear of the hard-core raunch which has become the norm in the music industry, record makers have an even more insidious trap for them. These are the so-called "safe groups," including rap singers M.C. Hammer, Vanilla Ice, and the group New Kids on the Block.

The greatest danger today is probably M.C. Hammer. M.C. is a nice-looking black artist who has even received play on Christian radio for his song "Pray." He has a commendable antidrug stance. But when it comes to sex, the wholesome appearance amounts to sugar-coated poison. On his "Pray" video, blatant sexual innuendos abound in both the titles and lyrics of the songs. As for teen heartthrobs New Kids on the Block, youth expert Thomas Jipping warns, "There is not a group out there in America today that is doing more to promote sex outside of marriage than New Kids on the Block... by their gyrating motions on the stage, by their lyrics, and by everything they do to publicize themselves. They market sex."[8]

Hammer and New Kids on the Block should remind us that every album purchased by our kids comes as a package. One safe-sounding song may hook your Christian child, but the album as a whole will reel him in like a fish, then psychologically de-bone and cook him.

How-to-Have-Sex Education

With the banner of enlightened modernism flapping in the breeze, sex educators rode into the schools in the 60's to teach children "personal hygiene." In reality these educators were the vanguard of an enterprising force of social engineers embarking on an experiment in cultural manipulation. The early method was to enlist unwitting and often embarrassed teachers in an effort to help kids learn about the birds and the bees. Yet the real agenda went far deeper than that. The premises of this campaign were these:

1. Dad and mom's traditional upbringing disqualifies them to teach their children about such crucial and sensitive subjects.
2. Even if the parents were qualified, the state has an overriding interest in directing the morals of children.
3. In our changing and sexually liberated world, children need to be taught the mechanics of "proper" intercourse. "Safe sex" didn't originate with AIDS.
4. Because "right" and "wrong" choices are not always clear in a complicated world, children need to be helped to define the "options" and see potential consequences for their sexual decisions. The hidden assumption, of course, was that moral truth was unsure and perhaps nonexistent.

There was no compelling evidence to back up the notion which effectively fired family and church from the sexual shepherding roles they had successfully performed for centuries. Instead, the rationale was philosophical and political. It was a coup d'etat against parents, children, and the church—a naked power play which remains in full swing today.

The Onslaught of School-Based Sex Clinics

The agenda of sex education hasn't changed since the 60's. It has only become much more entrenched, aggressive, and candid. To see the peril for your child, merely ask the question, "What have taxpayers gotten for their money with the sex education programs?"

In 1990 the federal government spent a staggering half-billion dollars on "contraception" education, much of it through the school systems. Yet after three decades the problem has grown worse, not become better. More sex education begets more promiscuous sex, which begets the excuse for more sex education; the two partners breed their kind like rabbits. One researcher recently told a committee of the U.S. House of Representatives:

> This explosion is [occurring] despite all the time and money that well-meaning people have invested in school-based clinics, sex education and safe sex. Over the last 10 years, a 306 percent increase in federal funds spent promoting sexual responsibility correspond with a 48.3 percent increase in teen pregnancy. [9]

In other words, when your child enrolls in the sex ed course at school, the odds go up—*way up*—that he or she will have sex in the near future—and an unplanned pregnancy. Why then do the sex educators keep whining for more money? Why don't they admit defeat and go back to the drawing board? The answer is that their plans *have not failed*.

Their target is not *less premarital sex*, but sexual "liberation," now seen wearing the new label of "safe sex." This is sex where there is no transfer of the AIDS virus, no coercion, no unwanted babies, and with a "meaningful" partner. The goal isn't to teach kids how to exercise self-control and *avoid* sex; in much of the curricula it is just the opposite! Sex educators in courses spreading in schools throughout America are instructing pubescent teenagers how to have "safe" and satisfying erotica. As part of an intensive study on Planned Parenthood (PP), the premiere sex education source for America's schools, author George Grant reports:

> Planned Parenthood's sex education programs and materials are brazenly perverse. They are frequently accentuated with crudely obscene four-letter words and illustrated with ribald nudity. They openly endorse aberrant behavior— homosexuality, masturbation, fornication, incest, and even bestiality—and then they describe that behavior in excruciating detail.[10]

And the worst may be yet to come. In October 1991 a national task force funded by the Carnegie Institute strongly recommended *more explicit, uniform, nationwide instruction* for high school students in the arts of sexual pleasure and the greater in-class exploration of one's "sexual orientation." That's also why sex educators are at the forefront of teaching the use of condoms, handing out birth control pills, and putting more "health clinics" in schools to service their "customers" without the nagging interference from parents. Thousands of these clinics are already in place today.

Yet the landslide of teen sex is causing many people to wonder out loud whether the system is rigged by abortion providers such as Planned Parenthood to *create their own demand using millions of innocent children as pawns.* Consider these interesting facts:

1. Planned Parenthood is the largest abortion provider in America.

2. PP is a driving force behind the laws that, in most states, allow high school girls to get abortions through the schools without parental consent.
3. PP is also involved in the dispensing of birth control pills and condoms on a scale nothing less than awesome.
4. It is a statistical fact that birth control pills and condoms are 1) generally unreliable in preventing pregnancy, especially when used by children, and 2) usually accompanied by increased sexual activity and rising teen pregnancy rates. This increases the demand for abortion, which is often supplied by...Planned Parenthood, the birth-control provider![11]

The disturbing question arises, Are the providers of abortion using "sex education" and "contraception" to create the demand for their own product—and getting paid twice for doing it? They are certainly making money on both ends. And they are proceeding with the blessings of school bureaucrats either blinded or intoxicated by the sexually liberated fumes of our media culture, and with federal grants from politicians whose campaign bills are paid in part by the sex industry's generous donations. And lying in their wake? The broken lives of a generation of children.

Selling Sexual Snake Oil

Carol Everett knows. She owned two lucrative abortion clinics in Texas and managed two others. Now on the other side of the battle, Everett states, "Abortion isn't about choice. It's about money."

When she appeared on the "Point of View" Radio Talk Show, Carol recounted the days when, as a "family planning" provider, she was asked into one school after another to give sex education lessons. Her favorite classes were fifth and sixth grade, although she hit all levels. Her classroom presentation boiled down to one point: You need to take birth control pills so that "if" you want to "explore" your emerging and natural sexual options, you can do so "safely." And if your mother won't provide the pills, you have someone you can come to. Keep in mind, this was all perfectly legal and taxpayer-funded.

"The next day," she said, "my phone would start ringing. Maybe these kids couldn't even drive. You see, I could look at the statistics that Planned Parenthood printed. I knew these kids were thinking about having sex. Maybe they'd never had it, but that sexual activity would go to five to seven times a week when we put them on a low-dose pill [that was known to produce] a high rate of pregnancy. . . . Our agenda was three to five abortions between the ages of 13 and 18. . . . The most I ever saw was nine."[12]

Carol's warning to parents: "We've got to understand that birth control sells abortions." That's one of the hidden reasons that abortion/family-planning providers are convincing many high schools to install condom dispensers in restrooms, and to demonstrate them in class.

While Carol Everett can't prove that this kind of deliberate connivance takes place nationally, she does know that the family planners would have to be blind not to see the convenient impact that sex education makes on their profit margin. As she says, "Wherever Planned Parenthood has gone in, the pregnancy rate has gone up."

Condom Fever

On November 7, 1991, the bomb exploded—and the fallout has been raining down on our children ever since.

That was the day basketball superstar Earvin "Magic" Johnson let the world know he had contracted AIDS, following years of reportedly unbridled sex with women in several cities.

The fallout was the renewed demand by homosexuals and the sex industry for more "safe sex." Soon condoms were being given away in subway stations in New York City, dispensed in high school restrooms, and marketed to teens on major television networks. One producer in Florida is even developing a fluorescent brand complete with a key chain medallion in which to conceal it. It will reportedly be marketed to 14-year-old boys.

Should you accept this marketing ploy? Before you do, you and your child should know the facts. Condoms have been shown to be notoriously unreliable in preventing pregnancy—and that has mind-boggling implications for AIDS. They have a dangerous material failure rate. Surveys also confirm that adolescents, even with a high awareness of AIDS and trained in condom usage, *still do not use them correctly* in the heat of passion. Most studies show a 15-25 percent pregnancy rate for women whose partners used condoms, and a chlamydia venereal disease rate of 35 percent.[13] Most crucially, teaching condom usage and sexual "how-to's" in class raises the promiscuity rate and increases the at-risk population.

This is bad enough when the risk is pregnancy or chlamydia, but it is absolutely terrifying when the risk is AIDS. The AIDS virus is much more likely to evade a condom than sperm or chlamydia—and AIDS is *always* lethal.

Faced with this evidence, it is testimony to the sinister commitment of the sexual revolutionaries that they would risk almost certain increases in pregnancy and AIDS among children rather than surrender the vision of the reordering of the sexual standards of the next generation.

The good news is that the public may not be totally buying this twisted vision. Following a month of intense pro-condom propaganda in the wake of Magic Johnson's revelation, a survey by *USA Today* found that 54 percent "said they were troubled that promoting safe sex sends the message that society condones casual sex." Ironically, the AIDS epidemic may still be the best opening that parents have to impress their children with the only solution—*abstinence*.

Is This Your Child?

Think about it. A 14-year-old girl is bombarded with messages from the media about having sex. Her hormone-heavy boyfriend is getting the same messages, and he's on the make. Adults all around are compromising.

It's summer, and school hours are cut down. There's nothing to do. An empty house. A cable TV. A couch. A bedroom just a few feet down the hall. Even with the best of intentions, just passing time can be dangerous! And with all the pressure, she has to admit that even *her* intentions might not be the best. (She knows his aren't.) But wait—what about AIDS? And what if she got pregnant?

But then comes the school year, where she is instructed in detail on the art of sexual pleasure. She and her boyfriend are presented with methods to make sex "safe"—no babies, no AIDs. She is presented with ways to make sex "hidden" from dad and mom. They don't even have to know about the pills. And if she somehow gets pregnant...well, there's a solution for that, too. The school-based health clinic is right down the hall, and the law says that her parents need never know.

Welcome to the world of sex education, American style. The professors are the media, feminists, and liberal politicians. It's in store for your child and the

children in your church, unless you do something to stop
it.

The good news is that you can.

Winning the Debate

The truth about sexual "freedom" is that it only
exists under the aegis of marriage. This is the freedom
to enjoy the exciting gift of intimacy without the guilt,
hang-ups, emotional scars, and social destruction of sex
outside the bounds of a sacred commitment.

So what do you as a parent need to do? 1) Understand
and embrace this concept yourself—not an easy task for
those raised in the baby-boom generation. We are all
stained by sin, and we all need to come to grips with
temptations and biblical remedies. 2) Teach this principle to your children from an early age. 3) Live this
principle before your children, showing your love for
them and your spouse. Nothing is more important than
the right foundation. From this base will come the
authority you will need for "the debate."

When I say "debate," I don't mean necessarily with
your child personally. I mean with his or her whole
environment—your competition. As with the problem
of alcohol and drugs, you must realize that when your
child contacts the world through the media, school,
peers, and his or her own sexual curiosity, you will be
engaged in a debate with that world over when sex
should commence for your son or daughter. In this debate,
your child is the judge and jury. Should she or shouldn't
she? Why should she listen to dad or mom, and not those
she thinks might better understand her world—her
friends, M.C. Hammer, or the disc jockey on MTV?

You need to give your child the best reasons to stay
sexually pure, or to become pure if he or she is currently
compromised. This can be done through a variety of
means: lifestyle, deep conversations, casual comments,

examples, and frank discussion. Hopefully your relationship of loving trust and your reasoned approach will
win out. But you need to start by spending time with
your child so that when the opportunity arises you can
begin giving the right input.

When the beer-and-bikini commercial appears during the football game that you and your son are watching, what will you say? How will you help him interpret
it? When your teenage daughter mentions a "friend"
who is being pressured to become sexually active, will
you respond with knee-jerk condemnation, or instead
with a compassionate but well-reasoned appeal for
abstinence? Remember, you're in a debate that you *must*
handle skillfully.

Entertainment Under Control

Here are five tips for tackling this all-important
assignment. 1) Teach your children wholesome sexual
values as they mature. 2) As you instill these principles
in your children, watch television with them to monitor
programs for sexually dangerous propaganda, however
subtle it may be. If offensive material appears, use it as
a springboard for discussing positive biblical values
about sex. 3) Put your discussions on sex in the context of
teaching your child a biblical worldview that encompasses all areas of life and thought. 4) Put your discussions in the context of a biblical view of how a person
comes to know Christ, and then spiritually grows and
overcomes sin.

5) Until the child is able to handle a mature discussion about sex, restrict exposure to harmful television
and films. Never let your children see a movie until you
know *exactly* what it contains. Many family-oriented
publications are now available which do the screening
job for you. I recommend that if you allow your children
to see movies either at a theater or at home on a VCR,
you subscribe to such a service.

But what if your child is already infected from past lax standards? How can you *remove* entertainment they are already conditioned to enjoying? My advice is to go into the "reasoned debate" mode, with a view toward cessation of exposure to tempting material and of sexual activity if it has started. You can't decide for your child, but confrontation, love, and a good set of reasons can make an impact.

The Truth About Safe Sex

QUESTION 1: What is the greatest myth about modern American teenage sexual attitudes? ANSWER: That most teenagers are going to have sex whether we as parents like it or not. In reality, studies show that most teens will opt for abstinence *if* they're supported by convincing education and strong, encouraging adult role models.

QUESTION 2: What is the most successful teen pregnancy program in public schools, private schools, and churches around the country today? ANSWER: Sex Respect, a partially federally funded *abstinence* program out of Illinois. It has an incredible and unbroken success rate wherever tried, and is similar to other successful programs around the country.

QUESTION 3: What is the school sex ed program most hated by the liberals, and most ignored by the media? ANSWER: Sex Respect.

These questions and answers are three great reasons why you should have your child's school, your church, or your individual family adopt a pure abstinence-based program such as Sex Respect. The results are phenomenal. Children going into such courses come out totally liberated from the pressure to have sex before marriage.

One high school in California instituted an abstinence-only approach after the administrators learned that 178 unmarried girls—20 percent of the women on campus—were pregnant. In the two years after the program, which taught nothing about condoms or birth control, the pregnancy rate was reduced to almost nothing!

Such examples are common. Many courses even have a "second virginity" program for teens who are already compromised. The curriculum is so down-to-earth and refreshing that you'll wonder why any school has anything else—until you remember why the sex educators are in business.

I can't say it any more strongly: If your child's public school doesn't have an abstinence-only program, the odds are high that your child is being subverted. Abstinence as a *part* of the curriculum isn't enough; usually it is just given lip service before getting into the "real" material. *Find out what is actually being taught. Read the material yourself.* If you find trouble, pull your child out immediately and pursue an alternative, such as obtaining material and teaching your child on your own. Don't wait to one day discover that a high school counselor arranged for your daughter to have an abortion you never knew about it.

RESOURCES

Books specifically about sexual promiscuity, sex education, AIDS, and abstinence training:

> *Grand Illusions: The Legacy of Planned Parenthood,* by George Grant (Wolgemuth & Hyatt, 1989)
> *AIDS—What the Government Isn't Telling You,* by Dr. Lorraine Day, 1991
> Books on teen sexuality by Josh McDowell (Here's Life Publishers)

Organizations:

> Project Respect, P.O. Box 97, Golf, Illinois 60029-0097

CHAPTER EIGHT

Why Gay
Is Not Happy

*Do you realize that 12 percent of the little boys
and girls in this country will be homosexual? ... We will protect our children!*[1]
          —Robin Tyler
           gay activist, at a
           Washington D.C. rally

*The problem of homosexuality among Chris-
tians is one of the church's best-kept secrets.*[2]
          —Joe Dallas
           President of Exodus
           International

When no one else was home, he finally made the call.
He had to do something.

Troubling feelings of attraction toward men had
happened two or three times in the past four months.

Even though at age 15 his passion for the opposite sex was undeniable, these other instances, though few, had clearly occurred.

He knew he couldn't ask his parents. For as long as he could remember, his father was too hurried to talk to him about much of anything important. And his mother would only "turn up the volume" and insist he go to Sunday *evening* services, too. No, talking to his parents was out of the question.

But now, he was convinced God had sent him help.

Living in Miami, he was calling "The Link," Dade County's 24-hour counseling and referral hotline, which he had heard mentioned at school. The Link was there for kids with questions on problems like homosexuality, drugs, and teen pregnancy. It was funded by groups like the United Way and a local Public Broadcasting TV channel.

He dialed the number, and waited. Now, at last, someone would tell him how to get rid of those thoughts! Now someone could tell him how to become a real man!

He held his breath as the phone was answered and the recording of a strong, masculine, compassionate voice came over the line. It began, "Whatever you have heard about homosexuality, chances are it wasn't very accurate. There is so much misunderstanding about this minority group. Yes, that's what it is. A nonethnic, nonracial minority group.

"Maybe you hear other kids using words like 'queer,' 'faggot,' or 'dike,' or perhaps you are afraid of your own sexual feelings. If these issues are troubling you, we're glad you called..."

For the next several minutes, the voice went on to calmly, rationally explain to him that possibly 10 percent of the population was homosexual or bisexual. It told him that sexuality is preprogrammed in the womb—"Sexual orientation is not a choice, it's a given"—and that it was as natural "as being left-handed." Some backward members of society had not yet accepted this fact, and were suffering from a mental condition diagnosed as "homophobia."

The voice explained what words like "gay" and "lesbian" meant, and how people of the same sex commonly had loving, caring relationships with each other—and that they were normal-looking people who could be found throughout society, people who were perhaps just a little afraid to admit their wonderful secret.

"But that can't be!" he thought. Didn't his church teach against homosexuality? Wasn't there something in the Bible about it?

The voice continued, "One excuse for this hatred [homophobia] is sometimes attributed to a particular interpretation of the Bible. However, there are biblical scholars who say there is no cause for discrimination against homosexuals based on the Scriptures. Almost every major religion has a support group for gays and lesbians among them."

"What? Wow!"

The voice even recommended a reference book on the *Christian* perspective of homosexuality. He quickly scribbled down the name and publisher.

The voice went on reassuring him about prejudices, fears, taking responsibility for one's own desires and lifestyle, and "respecting yourself if you feel you may be homosexual." And it told him how he could get further information and help, because his problem may have been that he was suppressing his true sexual orientation all along. With help, this could be overcome.

When he put the phone down, he felt flushed and a little afraid. But he also felt something else—like a great cloud was beginning to burn away, a cloud he hadn't realized until now might be there. Was this a whole new world opening before him? It seemed all wrong. And yet...these people, this voice...it seemed so persuasive.

He sat quietly, looking out the window, and pondered.

• • •

The story itself is fictional, but the Dade County "Link" is real, including the excerpts quoted from the message on homosexuality. The Link gets thousands of phone calls every week.

How do you prevent your child from being in the position of this youngster? And if he or she is in this position, how do you cope? And finally, what can you do if your son or daughter has already crossed the line?

Overhauling Straight America

Make no mistake about it: The homosexual movement in America is serious about recruiting your child. While some target the very young (as we shall see in the next chapter), the main focus has been on young men and women from junior high age through early adulthood.

Homosexuality has been around since before Sodom and Gomorrah. It is a rebellious and unnatural disposition that not only craves sex with the wrong gender, but studies have shown that it craves sex in unnatural *quantities* as well—what some today call sexual addiction. And it has always been populated with those attracted to young males and females. There is, after all, no other way for homosexuals to reproduce their kind.

Not all homosexuals are planning to recruit your child. But "the movement" as a whole is very interested in doing so. And "the movement" is becoming more and more a driving element in homosexual culture today.

Indeed, homosexuality in America is a social sector which is becoming increasingly radicalized, aggressive, and hedonistic. And that has heavy implications for your children and your family.

Here are excerpts from an article published in the op-ed page of Boston's *Gay Community News* in 1987. It is a gay "fantasy," penned by Michael Swift, a poet and activist. He declares:

> We shall sodomize your sons, emblems of your feeble masculinity, of your shallow dreams and vulgar lies. We shall seduce them in your schools, in your dormitories, in your gymnasiums, in your locker rooms.... Your sons shall become our minions and do our bidding. They will be recast in our image. They will come to crave and adore us....

> All laws banning homosexual activity will be revoked. Instead legislation shall be passed which engenders love between men....

> The family unit—spawning ground of lies, betrayals, mediocrity, hypocrisy and violence, will be abolished. All churches who condemn us will be closed.[3]

The homosexual game plan is termed by one gay rights group as "overhauling straight America." Lou Sheldon, President of the Traditional Values Coalition, said, "They want to talk about gayness as loudly and as often as possible. The principle behind this is that any behavior looks normal if people are exposed to it over a long enough period of time."

The campaign is being fought in the realms of the media, education, religion, and politics. And even though homosexuals are a microscopic portion of all Americans, they boast media sympathy, educational inroads, and

the ninth-largest lobbying force in the nation's capital!
They are exerting an incredible amount of leverage
toward the fulfilling of their fantasy.

One of their most powerful weapons is propaganda.
There are several myths that must be overcome in the
battle against homosexual deception. Here are the most
dangerous ones.

Myth 1: Homosexuality Is 10 to 12 Percent of the Population

This inflated estimate stems from the often-cited,
but badly flawed, sex studies by Alfred Kinsey in 1948
and 1952. This research alleged that 10 percent of males
were confirmed homosexuals, with perhaps a third of
the male population being latent gays. The problem is
that contemporary critics have charged that a dispro-
portionate sample came from gay bars, prisons, and sex
deviants! More recent data, with much better survey
methods, paints a very different picture.

For example, the National Opinion Research Center
of the University of Chicago released a study at the 1990
meeting of the American Association of the Advancement of Science which estimated that active homosexuals *and* bisexuals were *at most* 1.5 percent of the
population. Other surveys have tended to confirm this
figure. Will you hear about these in the media? Don't
hold your breath.[4]

Myth 2: Homosexuals Are Born That Way

One young lady, a professing evangelical Christian,
called my talk show claiming that she had "discovered"
she was lesbian while at college. You never "become"
homosexual, she said. You always "find out" that you
were innately homosexual all along. That's the party
line.

Yet no conclusive genetic, biological, or behavioral
evidence has ever been found to substantiate this claim.

There is, on the other hand, impressive evidence showing that homosexuals are the product of external factors which predispose them to making freewill choices which are both immoral and self-destructive.

You will occasionally see much being made in the press about some "startling" or "enlightening" research suggesting a biological link. But on closer examination, all such reports have not been replicable or have been guilty of poor reasoning. This includes the 1991 "finding" by a homosexual neurobiologist who allegedly found a slight difference in the brains of a small group of homosexual and heterosexual cadavers (see endnote).[5] It wasn't surprising to see that the strong scientific objections to the study never made the headlines. What is tragic, however, is that the objections probably won't be included in the public school sex education course texts that will undoubtedly mention this study in a further effort to brainwash your child.

But what *if* someone someday found a biological link to homosexuality? Would that validate the gay rights movement? Not at all, according to Joe Dallas, President of Exodus International and an "exit counselor" to homosexuals fleeing their lifestyle. In his view, the key word is *predisposition*. A person may be genetically or even socially predisposed to a certain act without being compelled to commit that act. Fingernail-chewing, alcoholism, and temper tantrums are all examples. A person still has a free will, and needs to be encouraged to do the right thing.

Myth 3: Homosexuals Cannot Change

The simple refutation to this myth is that many homosexuals *are* changing—changing not only their behavior, but their desires as well. Christian ministries all over America are helping thousands of ex-homosexuals annually who leave homosexuality. And plenty of psychiatric case histories—*thousands* of them—are additional testimony to the fact that homosexuality is treatable and beatable.

Myth 4: The "Gay" Lifestyle Is Fulfilling

The homosexual lifestyle will be sold to your kids as a sensual Nirvana—a natural expression of sexual freedom. Yet as stated above, psychiatrists who actually counsel gays testify to the tortured psychological drives behind the behavior. Before the salesman comes to their classroom or TV screen, here is a description of the lifestyle by an ex-homosexual that you, as a parent, and eventually your children should know about:

> Deceit and jealousy abounded. Alcohol was necessary to obscure the truth of what was really going on around me.... I set out to prove that the gay life is good and wonderful. When it turned out to be anything but good and wonderful ... so many, like myself, stay in the homosexual world rather than say they made a mess of their lives and must get free from it.[6]

How many partners do homosexual men have? Before AIDS, the most reliable studies indicated that the *average* gay male had sex with over 100 partners per year! Over the last several years that number has dropped to an average of ten, still a huge number compared to heterosexual averages. And what of the quality of these relationships?

The Family Research Institute reports, "Most of these encounters involved activities in which the partners neither knew one another nor exchanged a word, and occurred in restrooms, bathhouses and other public places." Consistent and reliable studies have shown that 80 percent of male homosexuals practice anal intercourse with its damaging long-term side effects.[7] And while lesbians tend to have fewer and less bizarre liaisons, psychologists report that the self-destructive emotional dependence is just as real.

The grim reality about homosexuality is that ultimately *it is not fulfilling*. The evidence is that, like most sin, it can at best provide a temporary "high" which must be replaced by still another, until wrong decisions trigger the painful process of addiction, mental torture, and physical abuse.

These are difficult facts to confront. Yet they are facts you may need in the competition for your child's sexual identity. Keep in mind that you're competing with an impressive array of psychological and media-generated propaganda and mythology when it comes to the homosexual assault on the mind of a young person today. Probably the best preventive medicine will be the truth.

Myth 5: The Bible Condones Homosexuality

The simple fact is that the Bible unequivocally condemns homosexuality for any reason. Of course, this has been lost in the cacophony of mainline Protestant churches (and some Catholics) who are openly beginning to praise homosexuality and even ordain gay ministers.

Indeed, the religious delusion was epitomized by a distressed man from Pittsburgh who called "Point of View" one afternoon in 1990. He was Catholic, although he could have been from any mainline Protestant denomination. He said he had picked up a book in the vestibule of his church entitled *Sex and the Teenager: Choices and Decisions*. It was published with church approval.

Quickly flipping through its pages, he thought it looked good. In fact, it was exactly the kind of book for which he had been searching. He stated, "As I picked it up and looked through the first chapters, I was rather pleased with the book. I was going to take it home and give it to my 15-year-old son and have him read it." That was until he got to the part about "sexual choices."

The reality was that this book, endorsed by church officials in his area, promoted "a non-choice sexual orientation"! In other words, it endorsed the fundamental pro-gay mythology, including experimentation to find one's own natural expression of sexuality. Yet it is exactly the kind of sexual booby trap that many Christian parents face every day in our souring culture.

So what *does* the Bible say? Passages against homosexuality abound in both the Old and New Testament. Romans 1 portrays it as a sin which is a key aspect of a domino effect of social depravity which entails harsh judgment. The biblical reason for this attention to homosexuality is that it is unnatural. It flies in the face of a primary dynamic of God's creation. Unlike celibacy, homosexuality is a total reversal of the most important of human roles. Yet gay "evangelicals" still attempt to avoid this obvious point.

Many seek to present the biblical injunctions against homosexuality as referring only to homosexual prostitution, not monogamous, "meaningful" homosexual marriage. Yet the context of Romans 1 says nothing of the kind. Such an absence would imply that the condemnation is universal, not limited. Also, sex of any kind is condoned in the Bible only within marriage, and marriage is always explicitly described as heterosexual by original design. For a thorough refutation of the "evangelical" gay position, I recommend the appendix on that topic in *Desires in Conflict*, by Joe Dallas (Harvest House). You need to become familiar with this material, and as your children mature you need to incorporate it into their biblical education.

Homosexuality will become an increasingly heated topic in the 90's, and your family needs the anchor of the

Scriptures to avoid two extremes: 1) being "blown here and there by every wind of teaching" (Ephesians 4:14), thereby risking compromise with homosexual deceptions, and 2) adopting a stance which seems to hate the sinner as much as the sin—the "gay-bashing" mentality. Homosexuality is a particularly pernicious and destructive sin, but its practitioners need the love and healing of Christ as much as we need to stand against their attacks on our families. Teach your children to avoid both extremes.

How Does a Child Become Homosexual?

In summarizing the research done by various parties, we find that the factors leading to a homosexual lifestyle fall into two categories.

1. Unusual sexual experience in childhood. A child is more likely to become homosexual if in childhood he has a homosexual experience, or has his first sex with an adult. This is especially true if that adult is an authority figure such as a teacher, counselor, or relative. If the child is a girl, then sexual interaction with men is a factor. Pornography has also been known to be harmful.

2. Family abnormality. Other than a childhood experience, the classic psychiatric history of a homosexual male is a child who had a distant or even emotionally abusive father. Psychiatry has established this syndrome quite well. Virtually all male homosexuals in study after study admitted to a poor or even hateful relationship with their father. Their longing for a father figure they could love became blurred with the sexual sensations of puberty, producing homosexual desires.

How tragic, then, are encouragements and lies such as those of the "Link" line mentioned at the beginning of this chapter! Just when a positive guidance is needed, the recruiters descend from the darkness to stoke the passions of a troubled youth who might have straightened out.

Lesbianism is much the same. Counseling with lesbians indicates a consistent pattern of a need for emotional bonding with a mother figure to fill a void. The need for an emotional attachment with another woman is so strong that when "that perfect friend" comes along, sexual feelings blur into the emotional ties and lesbianism results.

Homosexual Evangelism in the Classroom

The school systems of America form a vast chain of institutions containing millions of impressionable kids. Once thought to be a bastion of wholesome values, they are now becoming a fertile predator zone for aggressive homosexual recruiting. Do not underestimate the seriousness of this threat. School curriculum and counseling almost universally teach that homosexuality is both normal and natural.

Joe Dallas is President of Exodus, International, a ministry that helps homosexuals escape that lifestyle. He reported that while on a radio call-in show in Chicago, a young Christian woman phoned in who was battling lesbian desires. Apparently having an abnormal emotional dependency on her mother that had transferred to other women and blurred with pubescent sexual awakening, she realized something was wrong and went to her school guidance counselor.

The counselor explained that she needed to throw off her "repression" and learn to "express her true (lesbian) identity."

"No," the young woman insisted. "I'm a Christian, and I believe what I'm feeling is wrong."

But the counselor was ready. She referred her to some "good Christian literature" affirming the propriety of homosexuality. Fortunately, this young woman had the God-given sense to smell a lie and found help when she contacted Joe and found out about his ministry. But what of so many others who are falling prey to the deception?

Consider Project 10. Project 10 is a curricula concept spreading through many school systems in America, originating in Los Angeles. Designed to affirm homosexuality, the title is based upon the "10 to 12 percent" premise. The sponsors want to find this mythical "10-12 percent" who are allegedly being repressed by traditional sexuality. Of course, translated into reality, what they are doing is recruiting children by planting poisonous thoughts into some and exploiting unhappy childhood circumstances of others. And all of these are children who, with *proper* help, could be normal, happy husbands and wives.

Project 10 reading material sponsored by the Los Angeles school board included the book *One Teenager in 10: Testimony by Gay and Lesbian Youth*. What does this book have for your child? Here's a "testimony":

> I was twelve. I had known my dance teacher for three years before I was asked to give a special dance presentation in another city. [My teacher said] I want to make love to you. She positioned me on the bed, with my head on a pillow.... using her mouth and tongue... giving me a feeling I had never felt before.... I became a lesbian and a woman that night.[8]

By the way, you are paying for Project 10 implementation in many areas through your federal tax dollars, much of it labeled "AIDS education."

That's why I wasn't surprised in early 1991 when I received items in the package given to teachers at a New Jersey public education convention. It included position papers aimed at indoctrinating teachers and showing them how to conduct in-class sensitivity training on the positive nature of homosexuality.

The training, called "Toward Understanding...1 in 10 of Us Is Lesbian or Gay" was bad enough. But the real shock came from a sheet from Planned Parenthood with a bibliography and resource organizations. A small selection of the titles included will demonstrate my concern:

FICTION FOR YOUNG PEOPLE

Annie on My Mind, by Nancy Garden. New York: Farrah, Straus and Giroux. The friendship of two high school students, Annie and Liza, turns into love.

The Best Little Boy in the World, by John Reid. New York: Ballantine. A boy's coming-out story.

Patience and Sarah, by Isabel Miller. New York: McGraw-Hill. Love story of two women in nineteenth-century New England.

NON-FICTION FOR YOUNG PEOPLE

One Teenager in 10—Writings by Gay and Lesbian Youth.

Reflections of a Rock Lobster, by Aaron Fricke. Boston: Alyson Publications. True story of a gay high school boy who comes out and takes a male date to the prom.

Young, Gay and Proud. Boston: Alyson Publications. Written by and for young people. Essays cover topics such as telling parents, telling friends, etc.

This is come-on material written to sway the confused youngster who has grown up with one or two strikes against his gender identity. Just when he or she may be beginning to cope with it—wham! Here come the wolves, with their seductive primers in sexual suicide.

Stopping the Recruiting Campaign at Your Door

Your strategy for protection will be to guard against the two categories of adverse influences mentioned earlier in this chapter, which typically contribute to eventual homosexuality. I urge you to review those points, and consider some of the following measures.

As a parent, *you* should take the lead in the sex education of your child. If you need to learn how and when to introduce these matters to your child, then you should consult a respected, biblical, Christian source. You should protect your child from all exposure to pornographic material, including so-called "soft" pornography. More information is available in Chapters 7 and 9 of this book.

Cultivate a warm home with a proper gender roles. Spend time with your children. Make spirituality a centerpiece of your home. Model a wholesome sexuality. If you are a single parent, find a compensating role model of the opposite sex for your child. If you are divorced, take actions to minimize and heal the experience for your child.

Stopping the Recruiting Campaign *Before* It Reaches Your Door

When you sense they are mature enough to handle it, talk to your children about sexuality, homosexuality, and why homosexuality is undesirable. Remember, you will be competing with a highly pro-homosexual news and entertainment media, so you need to be rational, compassionate, and convincing. Be careful about being too harsh or playing into the media's stereotype of the "gay-bashing bigot," a misstep which could undermine your credibility.

Monitor your children's school curricula in detail, especially sexual education material. When offensive material is found, take the recourse with the school and your child as described in Chapter 3. Talk with your child about the myths of homosexuality.

Finally, get politically involved in halting homosexual militants from turning the educational system and civil rights laws into tools for reshaping society. The homosexuals want to pass legislation which would legitimize their status and make their sexual orientation an acceptable option to our youth. Gay rights bills, laws redefining the family to include homosexual couples, and electing homosexuals to office are all high on the gay "to do" list. Network with national and local pro-family groups and put a stop to this overhaul.

If Your Son or Daughter "Comes Out of the Closet"

To see the dangerous extent of the misinformation being spread about homosexuality, just check the August 1991 issue of *Parents* magazine. This is a mainstream journal for moms and dads. Its circulation is immense and its trust level is high. But in answering the question "What if your teenager expresses homosexual tendencies?" a respected columnist, Dr. David Elkind, offered this horribly deluded reply:

> Even in this enlightened age, many people still see homosexuality as a sexual perversion or an illness rather than what it is—a *normal and common form of human sexual expression.*

Obviously, a faulty premise such as this can result in the wrong approach should your child face this problem. But what is the right approach? Joe Dallas counsels those seeking deliverance. He recommends the following steps.

1. Ascertain your son or daughter's feelings about homosexuality. If they're unsure or realize they're trapped in sin, you can help them seek the counsel of a ministry like Exodus. Should they be more stubborn,

your best strategy is to let them know you love them if not their behavior, to keep the lines of communications open, and to pray fervently.

2. Thank them for their trust in you, should they take the initiative to admit their condition. This does not imply approval.

3. Express your own feelings. Telling them they'll burn in hell is almost certainly a mistake: It may be what they expect you to say, and would tend to justify any latent resentment. Instead, Dallas recommends saying something like "I feel shocked.... Look, I can never believe that homosexuality is normal. That goes against all my principles." At the same time, you should resist the common impulses either to "fix" the problem or to angrily cut them off.

4. Listen. You need to let them tell their story, or you will never be able to communicate from your perspective.

5. State your limitations, especially if they live in the home. They have the right to live their lives, but you have the right to live yours, too.

It's a tough situation, but not hopeless. Thousands are "coming out" of homosexuality. As one writer has said, homosexuals do not need to be encouraged to come out of the closet, they need to be implored to come into the light.

RESOURCES

Books:
    Desires in Conflict, by Joe Dallas
    How Will I Tell My Mother?, by Jerry Arterburn
    Exposing the AIDS Scandal, by Dr. Paul Cameron
Ministries:
    Exodus International, P.O. Box 2121, San Rafael, California 94912 (counseling)
    Family Research Institute, P.O. Box 2091, Washington D.C. 20013

(newsletter, brochures, scientific and statistical research)

Spatula Ministries, P.O. Box 444, La Habra, California 90631 (helping parents cope)

Traditional Values Coalition, 100 So. Anaheim Blvd, Ste. 350, Anaheim, California 92805 (political action)

CHAPTER NINE

The Madonna Strategy

*The blood-dimmed tide is loosed, and everywhere
The ceremony of innocence is drowned;
The best lack all conviction, while the worst
Are full of passionate intensity.*[1]
> —W. B. Yeats

For us, too much is not enough.
> —Michael Swift
> homosexual activist

In the early part of 1991, Madonna released the feature-length film *Truth or Dare,* a chronicle of her 1990 world tour in which she simulated masturbation onstage and was backed by a crew of homosexual dancers dressed in women's underwear. As with most pornography, the primary target audience included your children.

During that tour she was asked by a reporter, "What do teenage kids from middle America think when they see men dancing together or wearing bullet bras? Are they digesting these sophisticated images?" Her answer epitomizes what I call "The Madonna Strategy," although it is hardly unique to her.

She replied, "[M]aybe they'll be unconsciously aroused by it. Maybe they'll be unconsciously challenged by the idea of men in women's lingerie.... If people keep seeing it and seeing it and seeing it, eventually it's not going to be such a strange thing."[2]

Beyond Promiscuity

Why do you need to understand The Madonna Strategy? Because plans have been laid to coax your child beyond mere promiscuity or adult homosexual experimentation. Today even more novel "freedoms" are being explored, and all the walls are crumbling. What was unthinkable only a decade ago has become not only common, but is persuasively sold to children as a sexual right. The strategy includes:

1. Enticing your child into full sexuality at an *early age*.

2. Enticing your child into increasingly *deviant forms* of sexuality, both heterosexual and homosexual.

3. Making your child *easier prey for molestation*, which often turns its victims into strong candidates for deviancy themselves.

How is it being done? Madonna, the master seductress of youth, said it herself: "If they keep seeing it and seeing it and seeing it, eventually it's not going to be such a strange thing."

It is imperative for you to know *who* is planning this indoctrination of your child and exactly *how* these people operate. They include some of the wealthiest individuals and industries in America. They have ready access to your child. They often work behind the cover of legitimacy. Yet like the little Dutch boy with his finger in the dike, you can hold back this entire ocean of depravity with a limited amount of well-placed effort. But you need to see the ocean for what it is, and where to plug the leaks in your family.

How Perversion Went Platinum

Even as rock lyrics are the dominant influence on today's children, so the dominant influence in rock music is sex. What you probably don't know is that bizarre, kinky sex is becoming the dominant type of sex in rock. One popular song, "Leatherbound," tells its young listeners, "The whip is my toy, handcuffs are your joy."[3] It's not an unusual image.

If that alone is disturbing, consider this new wrinkle. The sexual power of rock in the past consisted of the word pictures painted by the lyrics anchored to a driving, arousing beat. The power of pornography was found in the explicit (or at minimum, highly suggestive) visual assault on the mind, producing rapists and sexual killers such as Ted Bundy. Today, with the advent of music videos, we have both elements united in one medium. Eric Holmberg states, "Music today mainlines a graphic form of sexuality that's as pervasive as it is perverse. With music video programming in over 80 million homes, the average teenager today spends up to 2 to 3 hours plugged into these images."[4]

Thomas Jipping of the Free Congress Foundation has categorized the nine predominant sexual themes found in rock songs and rock videos today, other than pure fornication. His research found these themes to be: 1) oral sex, 2) rape, 3) incest, 4) anal sex, 5) sadomasochism, 6) lesbianism, 7) masturbation, 8) prostitution, and 9) sex with the dead.[5]

Keep in mind that these are not the territory of merely a handful of fringe groups with small cult followings. Songs in all these categories belong to some of the biggest-name groups and appear in albums that have sold extremely well. Their videos appear on music television every day. In all cases, pre-15-year-olds comprise a major part of the market.

The stubbornness of music perversion was put on display when the bestselling rap group 2 Live Crew was charged with obscenity in Florida. The combined forces of the television, cinema, and music elite rushed to their defense with the specious cries of "Censorship!" They even took their shrill complaint as far as the halls of Congress (where unorthodox sexual pleasure is certainly no stranger!). Yet what were the shapers of youth culture defending?

The album that got 2 Live Crew in trouble was entitled "As Nasty As They Wanna Be," which allegedly contained graphic imagery of forced sex. Two versions were released, one for radio airplay and the more in-demand "X-rated" version for stores in malls and shopping centers across America. A sample of the kind of lyrics (with the worst parts deleted) that the 15-billion-dollar-per-year music industry will take the most extreme measures to defend included lines like "The girls would say 'Stop' and I'd say 'I'm not' ... as you fall to your knees; you know what to do cause I won't say please...."[6]

How could such a thing become so widely accepted, even among a rebellious youth? Working like a sonic anesthesia, the beat creates an ambience which disarms the brain, and the lyrics inject a poison into the mind which shapes the picture of reality and the pattern of acceptable behavior for the listener. This physiological and psychological dynamic of music is undisputed by experts. And the results are being felt in torn-apart households in every neighborhood in America.

Creating the X-Rated Child

The entertainment industry's goal of seducing children into perverted sex at a young age is only an extension of a campaign that has been waged for more than four decades. The evidence shows that the sexual revolution didn't "just happen." Many authorities charge that it was a carefully planned and executed brainwash, and that the primary targets have always been the young.

In 1991 Judith Reisman, a former consultant to the Department of Justice, released a fresh examination of the sexual revolution. Dr. Reisman's work had previously helped authorities convict *Hustler* magazine cartoonist Dwaine Tinsley, creator of "Chester the Molester," on charges of—what else?—child molestation. Her latest research shows how an anti-Christian elite was able to reprogram America's sexual attitudes through the media, government, and school system during the last four decades.

The most startling fact, however, was the status of young people as a focus of the 8 billion-dollar-per-year porn industry. According to her research (and that of others) the realities are as follows:

- "Soft-core" porn (*Playboy*, *Penthouse*, *Hustler*, etc.) has always been highly geared toward the 13-18-year-old age bracket.[7]

- Probably the largest consumers of hard-core pornography are those under age 17. The stereotype of the dirty old man is being replaced by the X-rated child![8]

- *Average* first exposure to pornography in America is 13. And that's if you don't count MTV as pornography.[9]

The campaign was initially led by Hugh Hefner (publisher of *Playboy* magazine), inspired by the misleading data of famed sex researcher Alfred Kinsey, and driven by those close to the roots of the multibillion-dollar "soft

porn" empire. It was an empire built on sexual massacre
through highly precise and sophisticated marketing to
college-age men and younger.

These men would then carry their programmed
tastes with them as they moved into the influential
middle-and upper-class levels of society. Gradually, the
permissive sexual attitudes preached by *Playboy* would,
to borrow the words of Madonna, "not be such a strange
thing." The avenues to the minds of America would
expand further. Today the soft porn empire continues to
search out the young, and the massacre rolls on through
magazines, books, cable TV, and video.

How Pornographers Get to Your Child

Why have the pornographers targeted your child?
First, because children are easy to interest. Puberty,
curiosity, and a decadent culture are stream-feeding
them into the arms of the porn industry.

Second, they are easy to manipulate. Children today
have been called "wet cement." Pornographers can draw
any sexual pictures they want to on that cement, and
there may be no other notions of sexuality there to
compete with them.

Dr. Aaron Hass, in the 1979 study *Teenage Sexuality*, found that over 90 percent of adolescents surveyed
had read or watched some form of pornography.[10] *Playboy* was most often mentioned, although over 40 percent
of the boys and girls reported watching sexually explicit
movies or videos for the purpose of arousal. He reported,
"Many adolescents turn to movies, pictures, and articles
to find out exactly how to have sexual relations." He was
shocked to find that one of the youngsters' most trusted
sexual instructors was *Playboy*'s "Advisor" column.

What is it telling them? In one not-unusual instance, it offered a high school cheerleader tips on

increasing the pain of sadomasochist paddling. Other topics include, in the words of a leading journalist, "masturbation, buggery, penis envy, lesbianism [and] abortion."[11] Here's what some of the young teens in the Hass survey said about why they read the column:

> "You really learn a lot... in the *Playboy* advisor... I wanted to learn the real facts.... These magazines give me something to go by."[12]

> "It helps to visualize what sex can be like."

> "It helps me to understand boys better."

> "I like to read the articles to see what other people are doing sexually, to see if I'm right."[13]

Parent, you dare not leave a vacuum of sexual information or values to be filled by *Playboy* or any of the other lurid sources easily accessible to children today. Without your preventive training on the why's and how's of love, dating, sex, and marriage, the Madonna Strategy takes less time and energy to impact a child than an adult. There are plenty of excellent Christian books waiting for you to use. Whatever the age or situation of your child, the time is *now* to put your finger in the dike!

The third reason pornographers market to children is that they are more apt to become sexually addicted. Pubescent children are not able to handle the intense images of constant and bizarre sex presented to them today. As they review this sexually explicit material, the models of sexual fulfillment become permanent and the desires less restrained. And that addiction will mean a lifetime of money poured into the bank accounts of the porn industry. That's the reason your child is a VIP to the pornographer.

The full impact is clear when you know how the addictive process works in a youngster's brain. Scientific evidence indicates that sexual images touch off bio-chemical stimuli in the brain which are "taught" to produce bodily responses whenever this stimulus is repeated. If the wrong kinds of stimuli are presented again and again, a person is much more likely to make decisions based on those powerful stimuli. The Bible calls this stimulation "desire," which "gives birth to sin," which "gives birth to death" (James 1:15).

The tragic results are seen in the steps to sexual addiction:

Step 1: The child will respond to the perverted stimuli.

Step 2: The child will learn to respond *only* to such stimuli; he will be less able to respond to natural sexual or romantic stimuli.

Step 3: The child will need *more and more* of such stimuli—or more deviant and shocking material—to become excited.

Step 4: The child will have a tendency to act out what he has seen, watched, or heard.[14]

At best, the child—especially a boy—will be trapped into a life of attaining sexual fulfillment solely with masturbatory "paper-doll" images, either placed in front of his eyes or in his mind. His eventual wife will not be able to live up to the carefully photographed, air-brushed beauties in magazines and videos. At worst, the product of this visual molestation will be an addict to perversion, a rapist, or a Ted Bundy.

If Parents Don't Act...

When we aired a show on child pornography in 1991, one of the callers was a young man who elected to remain anonymous. He was a Christian, a somewhat recent convert, calling to warn parents about the mental minefield of pornographic images that can be an everyday part of their child's world.

He spoke from years of experience. "Here I am," he said, "a young man, still struggling with it. I just know there are young people out there like me also struggling."

On our show with Dr. Reisman, we answered call after call from young women whose husbands had been drawn into pornography at an early age, had carried their addiction into the marriage, and were now either urging their wives to perform degrading acts or were finding satisfaction elsewhere.

The most heartbreaking call came from a wife who for 12 years had lived in anguish over her husband's inability to make love to her, and his long hours spent, she assumed, with other women. For her, the reality may have been worse. She said, "He was masturbating in his vehicle while looking at pornography." For 12 years of marriage! Happily, both were now getting help from a counselor. But a childhood brush with pornography had resulted in over a decade of marital hell.

Are young girls immune? The evidence says no. And for them there is a double danger: They can be perverted themselves by the material, or can become romantically involved with a man whose ideas of love can only be fulfilled by escalating forms of perversion.

Whether looking at soft-core or hard-core pornography, your child's prospects for a happy marriage and normal life are slight if caught in this web. Boys learn that women are objects to be conquered and dominated in the sex act, not self-sacrificially loved "as Christ loves the church" or as portrayed in the Song of Solomon. And the girls, supposing that boys want this kind of relationship, become warped themselves trying to fulfill those unnatural desires.

Molestation: What You Need to Know

Yet the effects can go much further. Since the eventual step is the desire to act out pornographic examples, pornography puts children in jeopardy of becoming sexual assaulters, victims of assault, or both.

A survey of articles, letters, and cartoons in *Playboy*, *Penthouse*, and *Hustler* found approving depictions of sex with minors, and the portrayal of children as acceptable sex objects.[15] *Hustler's* "Chester the Molester" is only one example. In addition to these more subtle attacks on the sexual sanctity of children is an explosion of child pornography which most observers are convinced helps fuel the increase in molestation. The National Coalition Against Pornography (N-CAP) reports that as of 1990 there were 450 different pornographic magazines, 20,000 porn bookstores, 500 "adult" theaters, over 2 million videocassettes, and 165,000 production and sales firms.[16] A major portion of this material includes representations of children engaged in sexual activity with adults, children, or animals.

Is it surprising, then, that the highest incidence of rape victims are 16- to 19-year-old teenagers?[17] That the U.S. Department of Justice stated in 1985 that one in three females and one in ten males will be sexually assaulted *before their eighteenth birthday*?[18] That an overwhelming number of successfully prosecuted child molesters were found in possession of adult (and many times, child) pornography? Or that when major cities such as Cincinnati and Oklahoma City have enforced tough anti-porn laws, rape rates have declined dramatically?

Here's another bit of information that you won't hear on the network news. Whenever homosexuals make the case for gay rights and the "normalcy" of homosexuality, they usually attack the image of the homosexual as a predatory child molester. They will cite "studies" showing that more heterosexuals molest than homosexuals. The figure is true, but it's only half the story.

What they will *not* say is that studies also show that homosexuals molest children at a higher *per capita rate* than heterosexuals. A survey of all documented studies of molestation indicated that homosexuals and bisexuals have committed more than 33 percent, despite being only 2 percent of the population. In summing up this data, the report by the Family Research Institute stated:

- Homosexuals are at least 12 times more apt to molest children than heterosexuals.

- Homosexual teachers have committed at least a quarter of all molestations of pupils.

- Homosexual teachers are at least seven times more apt to molest a pupil.[19]

This is important information to consider the next time your school board, Scout district, or YMCA considers abolishing hiring discrimination based on "sexual orientation." Your well-informed voice will need to be heard!

Perhaps these figures explain the latest arrival on the scene of lobbyists and advocacy groups in America—the child sex lobby! Groups like the North American Man-Boy Love Association (NAMBLA), largely driven by homosexual activists, have paid staffs and a well-planned agenda. NAMBLA is the philosophical heir of the Rene Guyon Society, which espoused the motto "Sex before eight, or it's too late."[20] It is also an active arm of the "childrens' rights movement," which argues that children be legally equal to adults in every respect. One of the prominent spokesmen of this movement supports exposure of children to pornography in the public schools, as well as the propriety of incest.[21]

Are these child sex advocates a lunatic fringe? Yes. Are they a minority? Definitely. But this doesn't mean they aren't an imminent danger to your children or grandchildren. Incredibly, the American Civil Liberties Union (ACLU) officially considers *hard-core child porn a protected form of free speech,* and is fighting to enforce this position nationwide alongside attorneys for organized crime.

This Semester, Lessons in Rape?

However, your child may not have to listen to rock music, watch MTV, see an R- or X-rated movie, or read *Playboy* to have his or her mind wrenched into a pattern of severe sexual dysfunction. Your neighborhood school may provide all they need.

While in the White House for some meetings several years ago, I met with Robert Sweet, an aide to President Ronald Reagan. He handed me an article that came out of *National Review.* It had a note written on it in longhand at the top that read: "I'm something less than a fan of sex ed, based on what I saw as governor. This has fanned the fire." It was signed "RR".

The article was written by noted psychologist Dr. Melvin Anchell, the author of numerous books and articles on human sexuality. The title was "Psychoanalysis vs. Sex Education." Every parent should read his conclusions. He wrote, "The truth is that typical sex education courses are almost perfect recipes for producing personality problems and even perversions later in life."

He went on to explain:

> Contemporary sex education courses not only disregard th[e] need for intimacy, they explicitly violate it.... Sex education, whether purposefully or not, desensitizes students to the spiritual quality of human sexuality. In addition, sex courses break down the students' mental barriers of shame... which are dams that control base sexual urges....
>
> A vast amount of psychoanalytic experience suggests that the majority of adult perverts are products of premature sexual seduction in early childhood. Seduction is not limited to actual molestation. A child can be seduced... by overexposure to sexual activities, including sex courses in the classroom.

He concluded that explicit, values-free, "how-to" sex education could turn children into "mechanical robots capable of engaging in any kind of sex act with indifference and without guilt." What Dr. Anchell was describing was the outworking of the Madonna Strategy in the class environment—where, as he noted, instructions on sex are becoming increasingly juicy.

The basic advice for winning the war against deviancy is the same as given in the two previous chapters. Added to that, however, are some special steps to counter the onslaught of perversion threatening our children.

Make Your Media "Guests" Behave

As a parent, you'll need to meet the media threats from two directions. One, in your home with your own child, and two, in the public arena to protect your own and other peoples' children.

In your home, I strongly urge that you do not allow your children to have access to secular rock music or music videos, especially the hard-core type that exalts sexual perversion.

And what about television? Carefully monitor and restrict viewing. Especially dangerous are music videos which bombard the average teen for four, five, or six hours a day with perverse images of sexuality. Even commercials are following the format of such videos. I recently saw a Jordache commercial, played during a show geared for teens, which ended with a young man hungrily kissing the chest of a well-built woman as her dress slid off her shoulders. Would you allow such conduct in your living room by two invited guests? If not, why would you allow it in your living room by two TV guests?

To a great extent, no one is isolated from improper sexual input today, even the young. That's why your child must be filled with positive moral input. Nevertheless, lines must be drawn at strategic boundaries, especially when their maturity level calls for protection. Recall that the Madonna Strategy banks on its converts "seeing it and seeing it and seeing it." When the bombardment of sexual temptation becomes overkill, the Bible offers only one way out: Flee.

Is It Free Speech, or Pornography?

In the public forum or in your own home, you need to be ready to respond to two countercharges that are commonly made:

Countercharge number 1: "Censorship!"

As Thomas Jipping says, "The rock industry uses this empty argument because they have no arguments." The truth is that when you *expose* the lyrics and the filmed actions of rock entertainers (or, for that matter, the printed pages of the pornographer), their obscenity has no excuse, especially when it is directed toward youngsters. Free speech is not an absolute right. Courts have long held that obscenity is not a protected form of free speech. Columnist George Will has observed that if we can regulate pollution shown to be biologically harmful, why can't we regulate moral pollution as well, especially where our kids are at risk?

Your line of reasoning will be that some speech *should* be censored, and then explicitly show why the lewdness in question falls into that category. Have specific examples on hand when you talk with your questioning teen—or your wavering city council.

Countercharge number 2: "This really doesn't affect children. Rock music or pornography is only reflecting what already exists."

While mouthing the claim that their movies, literature, videos, and television are merely "reflecting reality," the fat cats getting rich from sexual corruption ignore an obvious and well-documented fact: What they show to children *changes their behavior*. If not, why would companies spend billions of dollars advertising through the same types of media? While it capitalizes on urges which may already exist, it then lifts those urges to a new level of excitement. Without this principle the entire field of marketing could not even exist.

The testimony of many parents, including those with Christian children, indicates that your teen may test you with these arguments when you least suspect it. Be ready. The odds are good that your calm but forceful approach will earn their respect, whether or not they immediately acknowledge it.

Teach Your Children Self-Defense

If your child is age three or older, can they answer questions such as the following? "What do you say if someone you don't know well asks you to help him find his lost dog?" "What if he comes to tell you that mommy or daddy has been hurt in an accident and has sent him to bring you?" "What if someone does something bad to you, and says he will hurt you or mommy or daddy if you tell?" All of the above are normal scenarios involving kidnap or molestation of children.

The strange but true fact of living in the decade of the Madonna Strategy is that young children need to be trained about what to do in such situations, which occur by the thousands each year. The best way to do this is through family videos and instructions available through crime prevention organizations and law enforcement. The best videos often use puppets or animation, and are as tactful as possible.

Experts say that all children, beginning at ages three or four, should also be instructed about "good touch/bad touch." Bad touch is any touching or attempted touching—especially by an adult—anywhere the child would wear a bathing suit (two piece for girls). The children should be taught that if such touching takes place, they are to immediately tell you *no matter what the person touching them says about the consequences of telling*.

Another danger to train your child against is "bad pictures." The most likely danger is that these will be shown to your child by other children. Not only is it mentally destructive, but it is often the precursor to molestation. Child sexual abuse *by other children* is hitting epidemic proportions, and the pattern usually begins with pornography. John Rabun of the Missing and Exploited Children's Center in Washington D.C. has stated that it starts with a child being shown "pictures in decent magazines . . . progressing to something in the form or fashion of *Playboy*, where you had partial or full nudity going on, up until something like *Penthouse* or *Hustler* . . . all of which [is] done over a long period of time."[22]

Sadly, these are the kinds of issues your young child *must* be trained to deal with in this evil day. It's becoming as important as teaching them how to swim or drive a car. Fortunately, help is available for every family.

Join the War for Decency

Did you know that as of the end of 1991, 60 communities in the United States were "porn free?" That Utah had become the first state with no legal hard-core pornography? That in 1990 100 indictments against hard-core pornographers had yielded a conviction rate of 100 percent? ·

Combating pornography in your community is easier than you might think. Many people have laid the groundwork for your participation, making it simple for you to plug yourself in and make a difference. Writer Kerby Anderson advocates these steps.

1. Get involved with a local decency group which is organized to fight pornography. These groups have been effective in many communities in ridding their communities of the porno plague.

2. Express your concern to local officials about X-rated movie houses and adult bookstores in your community.

3. If you receive pornographic material in the mail, report it to your postmaster and request that federal agents take action.

4. Do not patronize stores that sell pornographic materials. Consider organizing a boycott and pickets in order to get community attention focused on the problem.

5. Encourage your federal and state representatives to implement the recommendations from the 1986 Attorney General's Commission on Pornography and to use existing legislation to prosecute those who distribute pornography.

RESOURCES

Books:

Soft Porn Plays Hardball, by Dr. Judith Reisman
Kinsey, Sex and Fraud, by Dr. Judith Reisman
The Mind Polluters, by Dr. Jerry Kirk

Organizations:

National Coalition Against Pornography, Cincinnati, Ohio

CHAPTER TEN

The Party Generation

Drinking is acceptable. You see your parents drinking. In movies, you see people going to bars. You even see it in adult role models.[1]
—High school honors student from Chelmsford, Massachusetts

At 15 years of age, she was a high achiever who had won a spot on the school gymnastics team. Dad and mom, two successful attorneys, were proud of her. As far as they could tell, she had a bright future with everything going for her. That was until the afternoon she showed up for gymnastics practice too drunk to perform. Upon later probing, it was discovered that she had been secretly drinking for almost four years.

A fluke?

That would be a comforting thought, but a false one. In reality, the only thing that makes her story unusual is that her substance abuse was detected so soon. The sobering fact is that in America today, the average age of taking that initial drink is down to 12 years, and the levels of consumption are going way up.

A recent federal survey of students in eight states showed that one out of every two seventh-through twelfth-graders were drinking. At least one of every three drink weekly. One in four of these students typically drank at least five servings of beer or liquor at a sitting.

The problem was seen up-close at suburban Cherry Creek High School in Jefferson County, Colorado, where fully 40 percent of the ninth-graders admitted they had passed out or lost memory after drinking! Almost one-third could be categorized as problem drinkers, drug abusers, or both.[2]

The Signs of Our Times

Welcome to the party generation.

It's a generation plunged by secular humanism into the depths of despair, materialistic pressure, poor education and sensual enticement. The bombardment has now intensified to the point where getting stoned has become a holiday from hell, only to become a more dismal hell in itself.

Yet it's also a generation that can be saved, one child at a time. But it will take much more than "Just Say No" programs and a pep-rally mentality. You need to take ownership of the problem in your own home, and help others do the same. Most of all, you need to find out who's throwing this party for your kids, because this is your competition. Not only is our permissive and pressure-cooker world driving our kids into the escape of intoxication, but once they're exposed to it, media messages promote the escapism and many school programs offer the solutions that can actually make the problem worse. Parents need to wake up and take a look around.

Just take a drive down the freeway of any metropolitan area in America today and note the number of billboards offering drug and alcohol recovery programs. You'll find a smorgasbord of hospitals and outpatient care, including, almost always, children's treatment. As you drive, also begin counting the billboards advertising alcohol, or the billboards promoting your children's favorite rock stations, every one of which will be airing songs by musicians who have openly promoted drug abuse and who knowingly feed a youth subculture that subsists on the aura of altered states of consciousness.

It's *war*, and your kids are right in the middle of it.

When you get home, turn on the TV or radio. Count the number of ads begging you to "get help," either for your spouse, yourself, or your children. Then count the liquor commercials within a 60-minute span of any treatment ad.

That's the world your children live in—the world in which they will form their values. It's a crazy quilt of conflicting signals that becomes a pattern of confusion, leading many of our kids to eventually acquiesce to the drunken norm. And it usually happens right under our noses.

The Secret Life of Your Child

Not long ago a team of opinion researchers presented a list of five intoxicating substances to 402 high school seniors. The students were asked which of the substances they had used within the previous 30 days. The researchers then asked the parents of these seniors if they thought their child used one or more of the same list of substances within that month's time period.

The results are a real "smug-buster."

The study found that 67 percent of the students said they had used alcohol in that period. Yet only about 35 percent of their parents thought they had. In other words, half the parents of the drinkers *mistakenly assumed* that their child was living an alcohol-free life. And that was the most "encouraging" of these findings.

Twenty-eight percent of the seniors had recently used marijuana. Yet only 3 percent—*one parent out of eleven*—suspected this behavior. Thirty-two of the students, or 8 percent, had used stimulants such as speed. Only four of their parents guessed correctly. That means *28 parents of the 32 abusers* had no idea of the life-threatening game their children were playing! Six percent of the seniors had used cocaine in the previous month. Not one of their parents had a clue.[3]

"But," you may say, "at least my child is a Christian." That statement alone could put you in a high-risk category. Christian parents today are buying the myth that churched kids "don't do drugs." The truth is that churched kids drink almost as much and actually have used marijuana more than unchurched kids.[4] Yet churched parents are the first to erect deadly barriers of denial and false assurance whenever the symptoms of drug abuse start to appear.

To remedy the problem, we must be careful not to put on sanctified blinders. Rather, we need to take a walk in our children's shoes.

With Friends Like These...

What does the world of your child *feel* like? When the *Weekly Reader* polled school kids in the late 1980's, they found that by the fourth grade, one out of every three children felt pressured by friends to begin drinking. As the grade level increases, the screws begin to tighten:

GRADE	PRESSURE TO DRINK[5]
5	39%
6	46%
7	61%
8	68%
9-12	75%

One researcher states, "The commonest reason for kids using alcohol is that it's in the subculture around them. Kids in a grade school where everyone is drinking are more likely to drink. For kids whose parents use it, they don't have a reference point that doesn't include alcohol."[6]

For most of our youth, their "reference points" for reality are TV and music. Surveys consistently show parents ranking low when teens look for someone to lean on for problem-solving, although most say they *wish* their parents were more involved.

In other words, parents are in competition. What, then, do our competitors say to our kids about drugs and alcohol?

"It's Miller Time" for Your Kids

Think again about the "billboard count" and "TV ad count" we discussed earlier. Consider that the liquor industry spends 700 million dollars year after year to make young people think that drinking is great. Here are some other facts you may want to have in mind the next time your family settles down for an afternoon or evening in front of the TV screen:

- The average elementary school student can name more brands of beer than he can name presidents of the United States.

- The National Council on Alcoholism says that the average child sees 75,000 instances of drinking on TV before he or she reaches the legal drinking age.

- Depictions of beer consumption on TV outnumber coffee 24 to 1, and milk *120 to 1*.[7]

"But," you ask, "will all this really have an effect on my son or daughter's decisions?" Yes. Extensive research has discovered that young people shown alcohol media ads were twice as likely to decide that drinking was "attractive, acceptable, and rewarding" than those with less exposure.[8]

Are you a sports fan? Just for a moment, think about how many liquor ads are run during sports events watched by untold millions of children, and how the behavior encouraged by these ads is sanitized by the All-American aura of athletics. Consider how many of these ads are populated with sports idols, both present and past. At times it seems the only ones missing are those who have been killed while driving drunk or who are in substance abuse centers. One leading researcher comments, "There's a massive amount of advertising that tells youngsters that if you want to have a good time with your friends, have camaraderie, go to good beach parties, you better drink."[9] And they are believing it.

Stoned on the Rock

Since the late 60's, rock music and the drug culture have been inseparable. Back then, the excuses were "experimentation" and "higher planes of consciousness." In the late 70's, however, things became a little more honest. The issue was *fun*; the word "party" went from a noun to a verb.

Drinking and drugs are so much a flagrant part of the rock scene today that it seems futile to try to justify the connection. It's like proving that the sky is blue. The list of stars who have died from drugs or drinking just keeps getting longer. Yet Eric Holmberg, producer of the rock expose *Hell's Bells*, told our nationwide audience that the sex-drugs-drinking lifestyle is still tantamount to a "membership card" in the rock world. Without it, a performer neither fits in nor gets in.

It's true that recently some stars have spoken out against this lifestyle, but don't be fooled. These are highly touted exceptions, and serve to give the industry a false front. If a small number are drug-free, the rock scene as a whole remains almost 100 percent drug-enslaved.

What you must realize is that *drugs are a part of the rock worldview.* Drugs, like sex, *must* be a part of the secular rock scene. Rock could no more be what it is without intoxication than the ocean could be what it is without water. And when your son or daughter steps into the rock world—perhaps at a party or concert, or just by listening to tapes—he or she is coming into contact with the rock *worldview.* Whether they realize it or not, your kids are breathing that worldview into their minds and souls. That's one of the reasons even "good kids" get stoned. Yours are no different.

One experienced observer of the rock scene comments:

> People don't seem to realize that these stars are promoting a lifestyle. They're dictating a lifestyle to the kids, who say, "If this guy drinks Jack Daniel's, I'll drink Jack Daniel's." Yes, the band members *do* influence the kids, very much so.[10]

"But I Thought Things Were Getting Better"

Research by the National Institute on Drug Abuse released in June 1990 found that teens were becoming increasingly intolerant of users of cocaine and marijuana. It also tracked sharp declines in reported drug use by teens: cocaine use down 46 percent since 1987 and pot use down 28 percent, with most of the drop in the past year. Also, many more teens appear to be excluding drug users from their circle of friends. So it's time to stop worrying, right?

Not according to author and youth lecturer Jay Strack. While not wanting to detract from the genuinely hopeful signs represented by the study, Jay pointed out some major cautions. The heaviest one: Drug use is decreasing, but alcohol use is increasing. Compared to hard drugs, alcohol can look mild. But in reality its overall impact may be far worse than any hard drug, including cocaine. Drinking is "the number one cause of child abuse, spousal abuse, rape, murder, incest, and vehicular homicide in America. Almost 60 percent of prisoners are there for crimes committed while drunk. And it is a gateway drug. One of 7 social drinkers will become an alcoholic; 1 in 4 social drinkers will become a problem drinker."[11]

Jay also made one other observation. He noted that although marijuana use is declining, such a phenomenon has happened before, only to increase again later on. Pot use fluctuates, and there is still a massive amount of it flowing through our country at intolerable levels.

Drug Education: Just Say "Whatever!"

Unfortunately, the educational field has chosen to face the situation with the worst of all possible solutions short of outright drug-dealing. As with the problems of suicide and teen sex, their answer to the drug crisis is values-free, psychotherapy-based education. It springs from the relativistic mindset—the rejection of biblical moral values—that caused the drug and alcohol explosion in the first place.

One of the biggest such programs is Quest, in schools in all 50 states. It is sold to unsuspecting parents as a curriculum for drug prevention, character molding, self-esteem building, and health enhancement. There are several levels of Quest, including Skills for Living, Skills for Adolescence, Skills for Growing, Project Lead, and the National Coalition for the Prevention of Drug and Alcohol Abuse. There are also similar programs such as DUSO, Me-ology, Here's Looking at You 2000, and Project Charlie.

Once thought to be the showcase program for values-free "therapeutic" education, Quest has now become the battleground for a clash of worldviews. On one side are those who favor a biblical model of mentoring, discipline, and morality. On the other side are the "progressive" educational elite who cling to their superstitions in the face of mounting evidence of failure. Spurred on by a growing host of journalistic and academic critiques, a minority of concerned and angry parents in towns across America have braved slurs and catcalls in an attempt to halt the Quest juggernaut.

Exactly what is it that has so many parents so up in arms? The first issue is truth in advertising. The parents allege that the course is sold to them, as well as to their elected representatives on the school board, by the Quest National Center as a drug prevention program. The other baggage—far-reaching psychological and invasive manipulation—wasn't in the deal.

That leads to another objection: the highly probing, personal nature of many of the exercises. In a case in Michigan, Quest was investigated for violations of state laws banning personality testing without parental consent. It seems the citizens of Michigan thought that schools shouldn't be in the personality modification business, just the teaching business. Other parents have even started a class-action suit against Quest for invasion of privacy and usurping parental rights.

The third problem was the "values-free" procedures undermining the stated intent of the program. Although the goal of the course was ostensibly to get kids to say no to drugs and alcohol, the teachers' guide explicitly instructed not to state such value judgments! The theory is that if children are freed from traditional values and parental authority, they will make "the right decisions for themselves."

The Boomerang Effect of the Courses

Incredibly, the teacher's guide for a similar course mandates the following points of classroom conduct:

> No matter what points you eventually choose to discuss, don't begin negatively with admonishments about the dangers of alcohol.... You will lose credibility with your students.... Many people enjoy having a drink.... Set for our students an important model of tolerance and healthy respect for differences.[12]

The guide then goes on to have the students brainstorm all the reasons people would want to drink or take drugs, such as "getting high and feeling giddy."

Notice the unfounded assumption that if an adult gives a child a well-articulated argument against doing evil, the adult will automatically "lose credibility." In a day when study after study indicates the yearning by young people for a sense of direction and concerned care and guidance, the very authority figures that command most of their attention are forced by many courses to abdicate the moral high ground and draw the children into the trap of moral agnosticism. The confused values-free educators somehow believe that telling the children that absolute right doesn't exist will help them do the right thing.

The problem is well-stated by Dr. William Coulson, who helped pioneer such techniques and now warns school districts against them. He said, "What if Johnny or Mary's opinion about drugs is wrong? In [values-free] education it doesn't really matter... all opinions are equal. In that sense, no instructor is even present, just a pretend-therapist."

In other words, if little Johnny stands up in class and says drugs are fine, drugs mellow him out, drugs never hurt him or any responsible person, drugs are okay because the adults have their drinks...then Johnny doesn't get contradicted—not by the teacher! And remember, impressionable, on-the-fence Jimmy is listening. Your Jimmy, perhaps.

According to Dr. Coulson, Quest's own internal audit couldn't prove that the course decreased drug use. In fact, he states that these findings indicated that graduates of Quest *seemed to increase their use of marijuana!* The problem is that the high-risk kids will be encouraged to question and rebel against existing structures by all the "values-free" talk, and the fact that drugs are being talked about at all will pique curiosity.

Yet despite lawsuits, challenges, and controversy, Quest and its siblings continue to spread. Teachers tell me they're in almost every school district. The PTA and National Education Association are behind them, issuing action alerts against "right-wing extremists." The Lions Clubs International have even pushed them.

Like hundreds of other informed parents, it may be up to you to push them out. And you can.

How to Fight Back

The dynamic behind this war is a clash of principles. As I said in the beginning, ideas have consequences. Our nation has fallen into this quagmire because its principles—its view of the fundamental issues of life—has slipped. Because your child is living in this world and being influenced by it, the only hope that he or she has is—

- a home committed to a different worldview and lifestyle—one based on God and His

Word—that makes your child's world something other than a "hell" from which to escape;

• your awareness of the dangers of this outside environment and its damaging world-view; and

• the strength of your relationship: Do your kids trust you and your worldview more than they do the drug-pusher or their schoolmate?

Lesson at a Gas Station

Some years ago, when my wife Mary and I were driving from Texas across the country to take our four children to Disneyland, we stopped at a service station in Needles, California. It was in July, around 2 o'clock in the afternoon, and the temperature was searing hot. It must have been about 110 degrees.

After instructing the attendant to service the car, I walked toward the restroom, glancing at a beat-up, ancient Volkswagen bus with a psychedelic paint scheme parked near the station (a common sight in those days). When I opened the door to the restroom, the stifling heat hit me in the face. Walking in, I found myself staring at a man, about age 25, groveling on the floor and muttering incoherently. Half-undressed, he had apparently fallen off the commode seat.

Kneeling down beside him, I heard him whisper in a slow, slurred manner, "Hey, man ... can't breathe ... gonna' die ... need help ... can't breathe ... can't breathe ..."

I rushed outside and grabbed the station attendant and told him there was a man dying inside, that he said he couldn't breathe. The attendant just kept working and said to me, "Look, mister, these hippie drug freaks come through here all the time, every day. It's simple:

You see, when you fill up on drugs and alcohol, and then hit this desert heat, it cuts off your supply of oxygen. Happens all the time. He'll never remember it."

It was 1968 and drugs were "in" and parents were fighting a losing battle. I decided that here was a chance to present an unforgettable object lesson to my three sons. My daughter Marla was with Mary, so I went to the car and told Mark, David, and Tim to follow me, that I had something to show them.

When we walked into the restroom, the man was still rolling around on the floor—by now in his own vomit—and still muttering. I said, "Now, boys, when you think of drinking alcohol or experimenting with drugs, I just want you to see where it will lead you. Isn't he a pretty sight?"

After seeing the look of horror on their faces, I felt I had made my point, so I said, "Now, let's help this poor guy outside so he can get some oxygen."

This account illustrates the "gear shift" that parents must do from *protection* into *preparation*. In the early part of a child's life you must protect him from dangers by building a trusting relationship which includes loving discipline and standards. Because he trusts you, he needs to know nothing more than that drugs are outlawed. He is never to use them.

But as he grows, you need to teach him how to think through crucial moral issues. If he doesn't learn how to do so when you are in control of the situation, he may not be able to resist temptation when he's out of the nest. Object lessons like my gas station pit stop are never-to-be-forgotten, nonrepeatable opportunities to hammer home a lesson. And our culture is sadly decked with such opportune examples of the folly of drug and alcohol abuse. The examples are in your morning paper. They are on your streets downtown. They are in morgues. And they are there for your use.

Family Ties

This is a day when parents must reevaluate the place of alcohol in their homes. Parents all too often model the abuse pattern but give little input to discourage their children from following through on their own. Alcohol is in 70 percent of the homes of America, including many Christian ones. What about yours? Most teen drinkers found their first drink in the home.

Instead of modeling the wrong lifestyle and disqualifying yourself from speaking with authority to your child, live above reproach and then become genuinely interested in your children's daily lives. Build a trusting relationship with them that will stand up against the eventual competition—the media, their peers, the schools, girlfriends and boyfriends, and everything else that could draw them into drugs.

However, I'm convinced that in some cases more drastic measures are necessary to meet the crisis destroying our children today. It's a technique I call "preemptive discipline." An effective instrument in this strategy is a "family contract." Christian counselor Steve Arterburn offers a sample, modifiable contract for particular family circumstances.

FAMILY CONTRACT

In an effort to work well as a family and hold ourselves up as an example for other families, I agree to the following:

1. I will not use or experiment with drugs.
2. I will not drink or make a decision about drinking until I am of legal age.
3. I will attend school unless I am sick or with the family.

If the contract is broken:

First time   Weekend restriction

Second time   Must stay away from participating
                friends for two weeks

Third time   Family counseling

Son or daughter

Father

Mother

The contract should be reviewed and altered at regular intervals.

In our permissive age, where discipline is seen to be archaic and "unloving," some may view this measure as an extreme step. Yet no one today would deny that we're living in an extremely dangerous, drug-infested world. And it's a world produced in part by parents who have "loved" their children to death.

The Alarm Bell Rings

After all you can do, the wolf may still creep in. Here are some of the signs that he has entered your child's world.[13]

Subtle signs: Secrecy; change in friends; change in dress and appearance; changes in interests and activities; drop in grades; fired from job; staying out all night; possession of eyedrops; dropping sports.

Overt signs: Deep depressions accompanied by extra sleep; unexplained school absenteeism; mysterious phone calls; money problems; extreme weight change; new friends; rebellious; heavy-metal rock with pro-drug songs; acting disconnected; long periods of time in the bathroom; changing the subject if you ask questions; burnt holes in clothes or furniture.

Sure-fire signs: Paraphernalia; lots of unexplained money; repeatedly bloodshot eyes; dilated or pinpoint pupils, stealing valuables; mention of suicide.

Launching the Counterstrike

If the danger signals are flashing, how do you react? Express concern and love when you ask about these problems. And you will need to ask, *immediately,* and until you get a satisfactory answer.

If it becomes clear that there is a drug problem, you probably need to intervene with members of your family or "clean" friends in a group setting. Whether you involve the church may depend upon whether your child is a Christian. At the very least, you need to get help from one of the church professional or lay leaders for yourself, and you should definitely seek pastoral counsel if you think professional help is needed. And, of course, you will need to pray intensely and constantly.

RESOURCES

Books:
> *Drug-Proof Your Kids*, by Stephen Arterburn and Jim Burns
> *Kids, Drugs, and Drinking*, by Jay Strack

Organizations:
> Dr. William R. Coulson, Research Council on Ethnopsychology, 2054 Oriole Street, San Diego, California 92114 (for more information on Quest)

CHAPTER ELEVEN

Fade
to Black?

Life it seems will fade away,
Drifting further every day,
Getting lost within myself.
Nothing matters, no one else,
I have lost the will to live.
Simply nothing more to give,
There is nothing more for me,
Need the end to set me free.[1]

—Lyrics from "Fade to Black" by
Metallica.

The sound of a train whistle split the air. Frantically, repeatedly, the engineer blew the warning as horrified onlookers shouted from a nearby parking lot.

It was just before 10:00 A.M. on Tuesday, May 14, 1991, in Round Lake, Illinois.

Middle America. The heart of the U.S.A.

There, on the ties of the curving tracks, sat two 14-year-old girls, Julie Pallach and Susan Zingales, with eyes closed, hands covering their ears, knees drawn up. They died instantly.

What happened that spring morning in Round Lake shocked an entire community. But in a broader sense, this tragedy continued a growing American trend of teen self-destruction. Many observers suspect that such deaths signify the ugly results of years of hopeless secularism drummed into our children by much of our television, movies, education, music, religion, and general culture.

The issue cannot be ignored: Because preceding generations gradually forsook the time-tested precepts of Scripture, have many of our youth replaced the Bible's God with an unholy trinity of death, intoxication, and sexual exploitation—with suicide as the ultimate act of soul surrender? Have negligent shepherds allowed wolves to prey upon the flock? And if so, how can diligent parents today turn the situation around for their own kids, and the children of others?

Alarming Realities

The figures will stun even the most cockeyed optimist. In the past three decades, the suicide rate among adolescent Americans has tripled. *Each day*, 1000 youths attempt suicide, and 16 succeed. That makes it the third-leading cause of death among that age bracket. The second leading cause is homicide, also on the rise.[2]

Let's put this into perspective. Researchers have found that one to two thousand teens in America spend their summer vacation committing suicide. Suicide takes an average of 5000 American teens per year. That, in turn, averages out to *one teen every 90 minutes*! The dimension of the problem becomes even more staggering by factoring in attempts which are unsuccessful. For example, suicide attempts average out to *one per minute*, or over *500,000 each and every year*. A study at Cornell University found that 33 percent of adolescents surveyed in the late 1980's reported suicidal impulses, compared to only 10 percent in the 1960's.[3]

Boys are more successful than girls, although three times more girls make the attempt.[4] Dr. Michael Sorter of the University of Cincinnati Children's Medical Center notes that "the rate of suicide death is highest among white males. Boys will use guns, girls usually don't. Girls will usually try an overdose, and many times they are saved." He cautions, however, that "there's no specific profile that fits teen suicide. All children are susceptible. This is something that crosses all barriers, affects all economic levels."[5]

Crushing Pressure

What engine is powering this drive toward destruction? When you boil down the answers being issued by the army of experts assigned to the case, a common factor is *stress*. Another is *escape*—relief of the wrong kind.

The first problem is that society today has become a pressure cooker, especially for teens, and a growing number seem to be reaching their limit. The suicide note left by Julie and Susan in Round Lake cited too much stress.

Children in the 1990's are forced to grow up faster than previous generations, and deal with a maze of highly personal issues. These include:

- Broken homes and overworked parents. By the time they are 18, almost 60 percent of today's children will have lived for a significant time in a single-parent household.

- Violence—actual, and via television and movies.

- The sensual bombardment of an ever-present media that leaves little time to think about anything beyond its shallow, sensationalized messages.

Put yourself in the shoes of a child today. In earlier generations, children didn't have to worry that they or one of their friends would end up having their photograph on a milk carton as a missing child. They didn't worry about the prospect of being kidnapped off the sidewalks of their own neighborhood. Children didn't have to be so concerned about "good touch" versus "bad touch" by strangers or relatives, as they do today.

As we frantically press toward the next century, our children are living in a constant pressure cooker which can drive a naturally emotional child (as most children are) to make a tragic snap decision when confronted by a crisis. Reacting to the building pressure, many children are prone to escape, with suicide the chosen path for an increasing number.

Death As the New View of Life

The summer of 1991 marked the success of the book *Final Exit*, a "how-to" manual for suicide. It schematically outlined the do's and don't's of various ways to kill yourself. It was dubbed "a recipe book for suicide." To the surprise even of the author, *Final Exit* was a smashing success. Bookstores all over the country couldn't keep it on the shelves. Within weeks of publication, almost 150,000 copies were on backorder. By October it was on the *New York Times* bestseller list— under the *self-help* category!

Ostensibly intended only for the terminally ill, the sales of the book may indicate what many counselors immediately feared: Depressed and confused individuals, most without terminal diseases and who could be easily treated, would buy the book and receive encouragement and instruction for finding a painless way out of life. The most frightening prospect is that many of these individuals are our depressed and already-manipulated youth.

Yet the methods furnished by *Final Exit* may be the least harmful message it gives our young. The real threat is its reinforcement of the pessimistic worldview which has saturated our society for years. It marks another milestone, or perhaps gravestone, on the slippery slide down the slope of humanism.

The fact is that the wolf of secular humanism has run rampant through our culture, eliminating God, purpose, and hope. This wolf has attacked in the schools, the churches, and the media—and especially in entertainment and advertising. God is ruled out as a practical player in daily life. And while secular humanism has created illusory self-reliance, it has also caused a radical self-denigration. Man, once seen as made in God's image according to a purposeful divine plan, is now seen as nothing more than a chance spinoff of inanimate matter. Should we be surprised, then, that low self-worth is a factor in a majority of teen suicides and attempted suicides?

In a world where God is portrayed as a myth and temporal self-absorption is the new religion, perceptive youngsters will logically conclude that meaning and purpose are nonexistent, and that anything is permissible—anything at all, including self-removal when the pain becomes too great.

Churches—Havens of Unrest

Perhaps the rudest surprise you'll have is finding out what shaky pillars the church has become for anyone looking for help with their inner burdens. As the forces of secularism have torn into Western culture, much of the Protestant and Catholic churches have either fled from the field or deserted. Accommodation to liberal theology is everywhere. From the abandonment of biblical inerrancy to denying the deity of Christ, from embracing homosexuality to denying the certainty of moral absolutes, the glory has departed from much of the church, leaving congregations feeding on doctrinal and moral mush.

But let's not be too hard on the softheaded liberalism of the mainline denominations. Biblical illiteracy is making functional liberals of millions of conservative, "Bible-believing" churchgoers. Extreme mysticism, unproven secular therapeutic techniques, and utter self-absorption dominate increasingly in-demand counseling services.

What is the effect, in terms of suicide and its causes? Largely gone is the teaching about a personal God who alone gives meaning to the universe. This is a God who has revealed truths which are certain, who has credible answers to the problems of sin and injustice, and who offers your child unending joy and purpose. Also, in the past the warning of eternal punishment stood as a final guardian to those seeking relief in suicide, sex, and drunkenness. Reconciliation with a merciful God was held out as the only and ultimate escape from the problems of life.

Worse yet, we are seeing the rise of the occult in the New Age movement in our society. Occult games such as Dungeons & Dragons have been solidly implicated in perhaps hundreds of suicides nationwide. Along with this cultural flirtation with the dark side comes the concept that death is not a product of sin, but rather is natural and will usher *everybody* into a new cycle of reincarnation. To a hurting child influenced by this reasoning, suicide becomes a vacation away from pain rather than an eternity of anguished regret. Yet it's a ticket that today's deceived and rebellious kids are willing to purchase.

Escaping Reality

As the pressure mounts and the Bible is pulled away, our children are left to scurry toward escape hatches which often lead to the *final* escape hatch. These are portals which every parent needs to be aware of, and learn how to securely close. For instance, alcohol and drugs are one of the biggest risk factors in suicide.

"Alcohol is a depressant," one suicide researcher warns, "and at the same time, it takes away the mechanism to control our behavior." It also impairs judgment and leads to impulsive acts. Finally, the shame of having to face acts committed while drunk has been known to drive teens to commit suicide rather than face up to the responsibility of their actions.

Another suicidal tendency for young Americans is teamwork. For a teen today, making friends can be like shooting dice with the Devil. An authority on teen suicide recently stated, "A teenager or anyone in the middle of a suicidal crisis is not thinking clearly.... They really need someone else to help them." Yet so many teens are suicidally depressed that being transparent with a buddy often proves doubly fatal.

"Teenagers, unfortunately, turn to their peers for that help," says the head of Illinois' Committee on Youth Suicide, "and if they happen to link up with another teen who's feeling similarly, the two end up on a downward spiral instead of being able to lift each other up."[6] Does this happen often? Yes. The growing curses of cluster suicides and suicide pacts clearly show the contagious nature of the epidemic. Exhibit A: Julie and Susan, sitting together in front of that oncoming locomotive.

What Music Is Teaching Our Children

Like no generation before, this one blindly follows a beat. It is an army of lemmings on the way to the sea. And their music is beginning to sound like a funeral dirge. It's time we adults started listening, and learn how to change the tune. Numerous studies have shown that the *average* teen listens to rock music between *four and six hours a day*. Add it up! That's approximately 10,500 hours of rock music by the time they graduate from high school. Incredibly, the average American teenager will spend more time listening to rock music than he will in school.

With this kind of dedicated listening, the music will inevitably interpret life for the listener. And the interpretation of life presented by hard-core rock is both secular and occultic. The concepts of heaven and biblical salvation are mocked, and Jesus Christ is openly blasphemed. Indeed, the cultic religion that superstar Bruce Springsteen calls "the first church of rock" drills our children on a daily musical catechism of nihilistic despair. Its tenets include:

- Live for today.
- Serve yourself without regard or remorse for others.
- Pursue sex over traditional love.
- Exploit the darker realms of nature to achieve your materialistic dreams.

The rock worldview at once raises expectations for fulfillment and dashes them to the ground. It holds out the lure of immediate sensual gratification which, once attained, is found to be empty and vain. At the same time, it wipes the mind clean of desiring the qualities that make for a stable, fulfilling life: monogamous marriage, sexual propriety, selfless service, and a holy God.

Musical Despair

Suicidal despair is the frequent result of this ruthless manipulation. The main killers are found lurking in a form of rock known as "metal," with its subspecies such as death metal, thrash metal, and black metal. Their signature is a hard, driving, often monotonous beat, with loud electric guitars and exaggerated bass and drums. Costumes and symbols promote themes of power, evil, hedonism, gender confusion, and Satanism. These include snarling animals, skulls, black leather, chains, demons, and pentagrams.

The very titles of some of the bestselling songs are a tip-off to their content: "Suicide's An Alternative," by the group Suicidal Tendencies; "Killing Yourself to Live," by Black Sabbath; "Don't Fear the Reaper," by Blue Oyster Cult; "Fade to Black," by Metallica; "Suicide Solution," by Ozzy Osbourne. Is someone trying to send a message here? Keep in mind that these are all *major* groups with *bestselling* albums, and that this is only a small sampling. Death, including self-destruction, is a theme that pervades the rock music culture.

When you try to argue this point, many rock apologists allege that only a few groups do this. When refuted, they then assert that the titles do not reflect the actual lyrics. When your child gives you this argument, you need to be ready with some lyrics to prove him wrong. Excellent sources are the Parents Music Resource Center (PMRC) and Reel to Real Ministries (producers of the video *Hell's Bells*). Both are listed in the *Further Help* section at the back of this book.

Road to Suicide

As the chilling lyrics of the song "Fade to Black" at the beginning of this chapter illustrate, much popular music today commonly reinforces the key factors in suicidal youth: isolation, low self-worth, and impulsive thinking. Are they actually driving kids to take the ultimate step? A sampling of the files of groups like the PMRC would find hundreds of accounts such as these:

- A 16-year-old boy shoots himself under the poster of his favorite heavy-metal band.

- Yet another 16-year-old hangs himself from the goalposts of his high school football field while the famous song "Highway to Hell" blares from a portable cassette player.

- The grief-stricken girlfriend of a high school honors student found dead by his own hand says his favorite song was "Suicide Solution."

Perhaps the most revealing case was that of two 18-year-olds who had been smoking marijuana and listening to a song by Judas Priest. The song was called "Heroes' End." Immediately after listening, the two boys walked to a playground, where each one used a shotgun on himself. Miraculously, one survived long enough to testify that "alcohol and heavy-metal music such as Judas Priest led us, or even mesmerized us, into believing that the answer to life was death."[7]

Make no mistake: Our children will continue to believe that death is the answer to life until we give them a better solution.

Educating Your Children to Death

Instead of looking to God, children today are told that answers lie within themselves. Salvation has become "self-fulfillment" with no lasting meaning, no anchor in the eternal. Yet this secular frame of reference is what caused America's social turmoil in the first place, triggering the spiral of pressure and destructive escape. Nowhere is this cycle more tragic than the misguided attempts to attack the symptoms with the problem itself: the "values-free," "values-clarification" approach to youth counseling and education.

In order to "clarify" their "values" about suicide and death, students are manipulated in order to "get in touch" with their feelings. That's the theory, anyway. In essence, teachers have been turned from educators into amateur psychotherapists. Consider the 1991 case of Sunnyslope High School, near Phoenix:

Parents Fight Suicide Course

Arizona Republic, May 13, 1991—Teen suicide may be a mounting problem, but teaching suicide prevention does nothing to stem it, according to a small group of Sunnyslope High School parents trying to convince the district to drop the lesson from its curriculum.

The parents were angered by the death-and-dying unit of the required wellness course at Sunnyslope, said Marcia Cryer, who spoke to the Glendale Union High School District governing board on May 1.

The course "glorifies" death and runs the risk of encouraging students to kill themselves, Cryer said. She said the unit took students on a tour of a mortuary and showed a videotaped program about suicide that, among other things, depicted methods of committing suicide.

"Suicides have increased because death is taught as a glorified end," she said.

Death Assignments

This gets even more hair-raising when you find out, as did a shocked Department of Education analyst a few years ago, that literally *hundreds of thousands of children as young as second-grade level* are getting such "death education" assignments. These include writing one's obituary, reading copies of actual suicide notes, writing your own suicide note, and visiting mortuaries.

As a result of the courageous stand by the Sunnyslope parents, the Glendale County School Board backpedaled from the entire program. This is a positive example of what can be done when the shepherds are on the alert. I assure you, this is a reproducible victory, an essential one when you consider what may be at stake.

According to the values-free approach as applied to suicide, kids not old enough to know how to drive and often suffering the roller coaster of puberty are somehow mature enough to be taught to reason through the options—one of which is suicide—but hopefully choose not to act impulsively. The director of a suicide prevention association recently summed up her program by saying, "We're not teaching them what to think. We're teaching them how to think."[8]

This may sound "intellectual" and "progressive," unless you know the context of current educational trends and their jargon. Decoded, her statement means that children are often never exhorted that suicide is wrong! The determination of right and wrong, you see, is never 100 percent certain. According to values-clarification theory, the choice must be left up to the child.

And how are the children doing at selecting the "option" of continuing to live after experiencing such courses? The percentages aren't good. A study of high school prevention programs published in December 1990 by the *Journal of the American Medical Association* found that such courses not only didn't prevent suicide but produced "unwanted effects"—in other words, *increased suicide!* The Columbia University researchers who did the study found that those students most predisposed to suicide were precisely the ones who would be driven over the edge by the courses. They warn, "Talking about suicide in the classroom makes some kids more likely to try to kill themselves."[9]

That was precisely what happened in the recent case of a Michigan elementary school boy who hung himself after viewing a film version of the same type of act in a "values-free" suicide prevention course. The curriculum of the course was in many ways similar to the "death education" being force-fed the students in Arizona, at Sunnyslope. And it's not the only reported instance. In the film, the victim is saved at the last minute. In real life, it didn't work out that way. A major lawsuit is pending.

Parents, stay alert! Remember the heroic parents of Sunnyslope High School. And don't let yourself become a plaintiff in a case like the one in Michigan.

How to Keep Your Child Alive

1. Give your children a home. Take pro-active steps to cut entry points for the threats of isolation and alienation. Build a home of warmth for all family members. Budget regular time with every member of your family. Put a premium on unconditional love, which will include loving discipline balanced by unrelenting forgiveness. This will be especially important if your family moves frequently or if your work takes you away for long periods.

2. *Know your child's territory.* Without emotionally suffocating your kids, know who their friends are and what your children do for entertainment. Be involved in their lives and activities—Little League, Boy or Girl

Scouts, church youth, and the like. Talk to them *exten-
sively* about what they learn in school. Be explicit in this
regard. Look at their homework and scan it for values-
clarification and death-education material.

If you have established a relationship of open friendship and trust with your child, then these communication lines should be open. Use them.

3. *Know the warning signs of depression and suicide.* These include dropping hobbies or quitting sports
teams or associations; suddenly dropping many or all of
their friends; dramatic changes in the way they dress;
altered sleeping patterns; preoccupation with death and
the afterlife, even (perhaps especially) if part of schoolwork.[10]

4. *Master the misconceptions.* According to psychologist David Nicholson, the most dangerous are
these: Myth: "People who talk about suicide don't intend
to go through with it." Reality: Eight of ten people will
leave some kind of warning sign, looking for help. Myth:
"Suicidal people are fully intent on dying." Reality:
There is ambivalence between wanting to die and wanting help. Myth: "If a person is suicidal, he is suicidal
forever." Reality: Sometimes it's just a temporary crisis.
Myth: "Improvement following a suicidal crisis means
the suicidal risk is over." Reality: Sometimes we need to
follow up.

5. *Know how to intervene.* Again, Nicholson's points
to a nationwide radio audience are most helpful. He
maintains that the best counterstrategy for a child in
suicidal crisis is that someone, and preferably not a paid
professional, convey that he or she *cares* about the person.

Whether your child is in crisis or not, begin relating
to the crushing pressure in their lives that may be

driving them to this deadly escape hatch. Begin building a relationship. As youth expert Thomas Jipping says:

> All kids today—all people—want to be needed, we want to be loved, we want to find something that's meaningful to latch ourselves onto in this life.... I know from working with kids what a hug, an "I love you," and a "You mean something to me" will do for you. Well, these [rock] bands say it. And the kids latch on to their bandwagon. And unfortunately, that bandwagon only leads to death, to violence, and to hatred."[11]

Suicidal kids have a sense of alienation and isolation: No one truly wants to know or care about their suffering. This is usually a distortion of reality. *You need to break down that isolation.*

Other tips include: Trust your suspicions that the person may be self-destructive. Become available. Be direct. Ask him if he is thinking about killing himself. Use explicit language, not euphemisms. This breaks down isolation. Don't be sworn to secrecy. Don't offer glib reassurance. Don't leave the person alone, and assume he won't do it. Don't feel like you're the total solution. Seek family, pastoral, or professional help.[12]

6. *Eject the entertainment.* As we've seen, the lyrics about suicide aren't vague. That's why it isn't difficult to make a teenager face the reality of their horrible message. Press him on this point: What is the message? Is it a good message? Does he agree with the message? Has it ever hurt anybody? You might mention some of the cases where harm has occurred. Follow the steps outlined in Chapter 3, and pray unceasingly for your child if he is being influenced by this type of entertainment.

7. *Challenge death-oriented education.* Your assignment as a parent is to know what your children's assignments are. Don't be afraid to be a "nosy parent"; deep down, the average child will appreciate your love and concern. Look at their books. Go over their homework with them every night. Most importantly, ask about their in-class exercises. If their assignments include exploring the subjects of death or suicide, morbid or "scary" reading assignments, taking trips to mortuaries, or writing assignments such as obituaries and letters to the dead, then it's time to take the steps described in Chapter 3 to move against the school system and counter the manipulation being suffered by your child.

8. *Win the worldview war.* It is obvious that the roots of the despair felt by many of the coming generation are planted in the soil of destructive views of reality being preached by educators and entertainers. The three primary worldviews are secular humanism, the New Age movement, and Satanism. It is essential that every parent today, no matter what the age of his child, know these worldviews. In fact, the matter of poisonous belief touches not only the tragedy of suicide but all the behavioral problems seen in this section of the book.

Although you have an outline of these problems and some immediate action steps to address them, the *ultimate* solutions require delving deeper into the heart of darkness creeping over our families and children. This is the darkness of belief. It is to such battles that we now turn.

Part
Three

---

*BATTLES
OF BELIEF*

CHAPTER TWELVE

Cults: Rebellion into Religion

- *Your neighbors ask you if your children can come with their family on Sunday to visit "this really different church" that has meant so much in their lives.*

- *Your 14-year-old son announces that he'd like to start attending a Bible study at a friend's church rather than his own youth group.*

- *Your daughter says that new friends at college have introduced her to a fellowship that practices Christianity "the way it was meant to be."*

Any of the above situations could be a perfectly innocent, even helpful, pathway along your child's Christian life. Or it could be the road to spiritual disaster.

Cults and ism's are crowding the shelves of America's "supermarket" of religious options, many labeling themselves as the restoration of first-century Christianity. And the young, especially teens and college students, are among those most easily victimized.

Yet the cults also present parents with a marvelous opportunity. Their threat can provide a wake-up call which can snap otherwise-napping Christian parents back to the essentials of a stable home and vibrant spiritual training for their family. These take work, but in the end they are your ultimate defense against this growing menace to America's children.

The Cult Explosion

Rebellion can take many forms other than violence, promiscuity, and drugs. Young people will often whiplash into idealistic religious solutions that trade the anarchy of society or home for the iron control of the cults. On the other hand, the victim of the cults may be well-adjusted, but biblically illiterate—an innocent who falls prey to the clever deception of counterfeit Christianity.

But whatever the reasons, by the 1990's the several well-known cults had been joined by literally hundreds of smaller but equally dangerous groups, victimizing both adults and children. Consider these trends:

The fastest growing churches in America are *not* Christian. Those expanding most rapidly include the Mormons and Jehovah's Witnesses, both considered to be cults by orthodox Christians.[1]

A study done by the Southern Baptists in the late 1980's found that the Mormons are converting an average of one Southern Baptist congregation (282 members) per week!

Of all children raised in conservative Christian homes, seven out of ten will abandon their faith after graduating from high school. Many of these will end up joining a cult.[2]

The damage being done by cults is severe. Spiritually, the peril of cults is that they teach doctrines which are so anti-Christian that they involve a rejection of Jesus Christ and His unique offer of salvation. Yet the harm done in this earthly life is also great. Broken homes, emotional distress, needless guilt and suicide, mental illness, and religious burnout are all frequent hazards of cults.

I have talked with people who have been shunned by longtime friends for disagreeing with cult leaders over a trivial matter of doctrine. Young people have called my talk show in a desperate state of confusion due to cultic manipulation of them or family members. In the documentary film *Witnesses of Jehovah* (Jeremiah Films), there is an interview with a young couple who were *commanded* by church elders to allow their baby to die because of a bizarre cult regulation against blood transfusions. Clearly, cults are a major threat which parents need to help their children avoid.

Testing for Counterfeit Christianity

Cults work on all age groups. They can snatch children's hearts in the early teens, wait until college to get them, or take advantage of deficient spiritual training in childhood by recruiting them after they reach adulthood.

How can you help protect your child from the threat of cults during both the present and the future? Perhaps the most crucial step is to know what a cult is, and let your children understand this as well. The dictionary definition of a cult usually revolves around the concept of a closed-rank, doctrinaire religion cut off from the rest of the world. For our purposes, however, we will use a definition coming from a Christian viewpoint.

It is important to know that the Bible commands us to test any group claiming to be Christian (1 Thessalonians 5:21; 1 John 4:1).

What are the tests we are to use? The Bible gives three primary standards:

Test 1:   Do they have the right gospel?
Test 2:   Do they have the right Jesus?
Test 3:   Are they guilty of making false prophecies?

If any group fails even one of these tests, you have reason for great concern. Usually a true cult will fail two or more, exposing them as a counterfeit of true Christian belief.

Test 1: The Right Gospel?

The first test is found in one of the most important chapters of the Bible, 2 Corinthians 11. Verse 4 warns against anyone preaching "a different gospel from the one you accepted." This issue is also raised in the letter to the Galatians, which says that anyone preaching a "different gospel" (1:6) is to be considered "eternally condemned" (1:9).

That's strong language! What's behind it?

The "good news" (or "gospel") is that Jesus died for man's sins and rose from the dead, and that forgiveness and eternal life are available for all who believe in Christ and give up rebellion and self-efforts at salvation. Jesus has done all the work, and no more "good works" are necessary. The only requirement is trust in the One who has performed the labor. This is taught in scores of passages, including 1 Corinthians 15:1-8, Ephesians 2:8,9, and Romans 4:4-8.

Yet both in ancient times and today, many people believe that *good works* are an additional precondition for salvation. Such a claim exposes a fatal lack of appreciation for the depth of sin and the greatness of the work of Christ. Even worse, the preaching of salvation by works opens the door for intimidation by arrogant leaders and organizations who spell out the terms of salvation for their members.

Warning: *Many cults are now using the term "born again."* Many are also claiming to be "saved by grace through faith, not of works." Yet in almost every case, the terms and phrases for faith are *redefined* by the cult so that what they really mean is salvation by works! Your question to any suspect group should be, *"List* all the things that God requires of me as a condition for being granted eternal life." If the answer is more than "Trust in Christ on the basis of His atoning death and resurrection," then you should suspect a problem.

Test 2: The Right Jesus?

The Bible says, "If someone comes to you and preaches *a Jesus other than the Jesus we preached,"* then that person is a false apostle sent by Satan (2 Corinthians 11:4,13).

When your kids walk into the world of religious options, they will find that the name "Jesus" has become an advertising slogan for false religions of various shapes and sizes. For example, while calling themselves Christian, Jehovah's Witnesses teach that Christ is nothing more than an angel, and they offer ingeniously deceptive reasoning to support their claim. The Mormons affirm that Jesus is "divine," but what does that mean in their vocabulary? Only later is a Mormon convert told that Jesus is the spirit brother of Satan and just one of the many gods inhabiting the universe. The New Age cults promote Jesus as an enlightened human. He was the "Son of God"—but only in the same way that we *all* are!

Against these faulty views, the Bible clearly portrays Jesus as the unique, eternally existent God who added to His divine nature the limitations of human nature, in order to be the sacrificial payment for our sins. He is totally unique—the only One ever fully God and fully man.

When the cults make their bid for your son or daughter, they will avoid passages of the Bible which declare the deity of Christ, and wrench others out of context to attack this cornerstone doctrine of the faith. Yet proper comparison of all pertinent Scriptures leads to the undeniable conclusion that Jesus is God.[3]

The realization of who Jesus is should be one of the most exciting moments in any child's life. Sadly, our churches often dryly recite the words with as much depth or fervor as eating warmed-over turnips. What a tragedy, especially for children who might soak up this exhilarating truth if only they had a little more encouragement from the adults!

Test 3: Are They False Prophets?

This test is so important that it is found in the Sermon on the Mount. Jesus said, "Watch out for false prophets. They come to you in sheep's clothing, but inwardly they are ferocious wolves" (Matthew 7:15). There are two ways that a person can be a false prophet.

The first way is found in Deuteronomy 13, which warns against anyone performing signs and wonders who also preaches a false view of God. When the Mormons declare that the universe is populated by millions of gods who are spiritually evolved men, they are guilty of false prophecy. When the New Age cults declare that various religions worship the same God by different names (Jesus, Allah, Krishna, and so on), they also come under the same condemnation.

The Bible clearly teaches that there is one personal, infinite, eternal God existing simultaneously in three Persons. It doesn't ask that we comprehend it—only that we accept the undeniable evidence that this is God's unique nature.

The second way to become a false prophet is to make a false prediction in the name of God. This test is found in Deuteronomy 18:21-23. It is so strict that if a "prophet" correctly predicted hundreds of events but then missed *just once*, he would be exposed as false. Under the Old Testament law, the penalty would be death!

Joseph Smith, founder of the Mormon Church, in 1832 predicted a civil war between the North and South. A prophet? No. His "prophecy" also stated that the war would spread to all nations, would include mass slave uprisings, would entail earthquakes and famine, and would conclude with the total annihilation of all countries!

Jehovah's Witnesses have declared themselves to be prophets, but have predicted the arrival of Armageddon several times before 1990.

Yet remember that false prophecies don't have to be spectacular. The small-time cultist who says that God told him that John would marry Jane is no less a false prophet than Joseph Smith, when John ends up with Sue.

Who Do the Cults Recruit?

There are four basic types of young people that seem the most susceptible to cult recruiting. First, there are the *biblically illiterate*. How many biblically illiterate children in Christian homes are there? A disquieting clue might be the number of biblically illiterate *adults*. The famous survey expert George Gallup, Jr., recently stated, "That's the central weakness of Christianity in this country today. There is a lack of sturdiness of belief. There is a lack of knowledge of . . . Christian doctrines of atonement, redemption, and grace."[4]

With this backdrop, just picture a teenager trying to handle the smooth sales pitches of well-rehearsed cultic recruiters:

Yes, of course Jesus is divine. But does that mean He is not *created*? Let's look at all the Scriptures to see how the Bible *really* fits together.

The Bible says to love your neighbor. That's why no true Christian church would ever send people into the military, would they?

Walter Davis is a perfect example of this syndrome. Walter joined a cult when he was age 14. His parents were "nominal" Christians without much spiritual oversight of their son. Davis later recounted, "In my youthful enthusiasm and *complete ignorance of what the Bible taught*, I accepted as truth all the [cultic] church's doctrines and practices, and I believed sincerely that it was the one true religion on the earth."[5]

The second type of young person the cults recruit is the *irrationally idealistic*. Idealism isn't bad if it is grounded in a Christian understanding of the world. Without that, however, it can lead to disillusionment and a desperate leap into the false vision painted by the cults.

Douglas Wiskow, a former Jehovah's Witness, testifies that "at the age of 15, I left organized Christianity feeling that it had nothing to offer me in my search for the meaning of life. Organized religion, as I saw it, was guilty of ... hypocrisy, complacency, and inactivity...."[6] Wiskow was one of the many who have bailed out of Christian churches in their teen years and ended up in the cults.

Closely related to the idealistic convert is the *emotionally vulnerable*. It's an interesting fact that when present and former members of cults have been surveyed, *the majority* say that they entered the cult at a time of unusual stress in their lives.[7] As we saw in the last few chapters, stress is the mark of growing up in

America today. Faced with increasing pressures, children are more often letting their guard down and becoming open to any messiah who will promise to take away their hurts and explain life in simplistic, hopeful terms. Parents can often preempt the cults at this point, supplying their kids not only with love, but with spiritual hope based on true biblical discernment.

The fourth type of prospect is the *self-righteously proud.* Some young people need to feel unique and superior. What better way than to be a member of "the only true church" where he or she is earning his way to oneness with God?

Recruiting Your Child

Steve Hassan, a former cult member and now an expert on cult mind control, states that "people don't join cults. *Cults recruit people....* It is important to recognize that recruitment doesn't just happen. It is a process imposed on people by other people."[8]

In the plot to recruit vulnerable young men and women, cults in the 90's are using an impressive variety of gimmicks. Most depend upon building a relationship with the "prospect." This is the crucial step to selling the acceptance of doctrine and submission to the cult's authority. Friendship, for example, is a common way to cultivate young people. Hassan warns that the plan might include effusive praise and flattery, but the goal is *domination.* Here's a sample line: "You've got amazing spiritual insight for a person of your age! We'd be honored for you to be a part of our study group each Wednesday."

The appearance of orthodoxy is another tactic intended to lower the victim's defense mechanisms. Many cults, such as the Unification Church (the Moonies), have mastered the art of using front groups that prowl most major college campuses. Such groups all have innocent, positive names and missions which serve as bait to build relationships with prospects. One youthful victim of the Moonies remembers first being attracted by a display table for "The Ideal City Project" set up on the campus green.[9]

Doctrinal fronts are also cleverly employed. The deviant beliefs of cults are often hidden behind terms that deliberately sound Christian: "born again," "Jesus," and "we believe the Bible literally" are some of the terms and phrases which must be carefully defined in evaluating a suspicious group.

Another step in relational recruiting are "special events." Concerts, free meals, and picnics can all be used to snare the unsuspecting college or high school student. Eighteen-year-old Steve Kemperman left his home in Rochester, New York, for what he thought would be four exciting years at the University of California at Berkeley. But after being invited to a weekly free dinner by some friends, he was impressed with what appeared to be spontaneous "joy" in the faces of the attenders.

One dinner led to another, and instead of spending the next four years earning his degree, he spent them in full-time street-corner flower selling for the Moonies! And this happened even though he had not even been religious before stepping into the controlled environment of that recruitment "dinner."[10]

After the initial recruitment is underway, the process of serious mind control begins: Deception. Sleep deprivation. Controlled environments such as mountain retreats. An increasingly heavy load of meetings and activities that crowd out time for former friends and recreation. Bizarre rituals. Participation in trying to win others to the cult (a key mental reinforcement technique). Extrabiblical sources of "truth."

Any or all of these can be elements in the road to bonding with the cult. The best way to stop it is to never let your child get on such a pathway in the first place.

Protecting Your Child

Of course, the front lines of defense are a secure home, a vibrant church, and an understanding by you and your children of the doctrinal tests mentioned above.

But for true security even more is needed. As a parent, you need to keep a watchful eye on your child's religious associations. Make sure you know the names and characteristics of any fellowship group with which your son or daughter is in frequent contact. Make use of the many fine countercult dictionaries and organizations available today. Take nothing for granted.

Another wise measure of protection is that when you share with your child the reality of the threat of false religions, teach him to ask plenty of questions himself— not only doctrinal questions, but others as well, such as:

Do they have a published doctrinal statement? What are the names of all other organizations affiliated with the group? *Exactly* what are members expected to do when they join? Who are their founders and current leaders? Is the group considered controversial by anyone, and what are their main objections? What do conservative Christian churches think about the group, and vice versa? These kinds of uncomfortable questions will usually drive away the cultist, but bring out the best in true Christians.

Liberating Your Child

Bill and Lorna Johnson's 19-year-old daughter Nancy was away from home for the summer to earn extra money for college. Out of the blue, Nancy's alarmed roommate called them to read this note:

I have truly found my place in the world, Leslie. God has summoned me to be part of the
Brethren who are the only true Christians on
Earth. I have thrown away my blue jeans, for I
realize that they were part of my Satanic
past.... I am learning to destroy this vain ego
of mine that longs to be part of this wicked
world.[11]

What would you do if you received the equivalent of
Nancy's note—such as when your son or daughter
announces that they've decided to be baptized in Jehovah's Witnesses to "work out their salvation with fear
and trembling"? Or that they are becoming a Mormon
because they received "the burning in the bosom" predicted by Mormon scriptures?

There are several strategies you can try when this
happens. One is a frontal assault on the doctrines and
credibility of the cult. This can be done by using proper
biblical interpretation to refute the cult on key matters
of belief.

Leading countercult ministers advise keeping the
conversation tied directly to the three defining areas
outlined earlier in this chapter—the gospel, the nature
of Christ, and false prophecy. This prevents the indoctri-
nated cult member from jumping from subject to subject
to avoid having his new worldview begin to crack. These
ministers also advocate studying the cult's teaching to
discover which Bible verses they will misuse to prop up
their position.

Another method of carrying out a frontal assault is
to use documented evidence of such embarrassing cultic
blunders as false prophecies or ridiculous statements of
cult leaders. Often, the person trapped in the cult will
not respond to biblical reasoning because he or she
trusts the authority of his leaders no matter how
twisted the interpretation of Scripture. This means that

you must first undermine confidence in that authority with outside documentation.

The frontal assault can backfire, however, especially when used by a parent with his own child. Often the son or daughter will interpret this as an attempt at parental suppression, and actually be driven farther into the cult. The better your arguments, the more defensive they may become. Accusing your child of being "brainwashed" can make matters worse. This heightens the persecution complex which the cult has implanted, and allows them more control each time you mount another attack.

What, in this case, is the solution?

Opening Your Child's Closed Mind

If you feel the frontal assault may boomerang, the key may be to delay confronting the doctrinal issues until other strategies are attempted first. These other strategies are all aimed at opening the mind of the brainwashed cult member so that information hostile to his cult can be seriously entertained.

What *not* to do can be important here. Instead of acting rashly by attacking, work on building bridges. Keep in contact if possible, and communicate love (without, of course, implying approval of your child's decision to join the cult). At the same time, begin researching the cult, especially its beliefs, organization, and recruitment methods. It is wise to get help from a Christian expert in the cults, even if it means calling long distance to one of the outstanding ministries in the field.

After researching the cult and marshaling help and prayer support, it is time to begin the intervention. Depending on the situation, it may be a gradual process over months or even years, or it could be more direct.

According to experts such as Hassan, cultic brainwashing is a three-step process. Step 1 is "unfreezing."

All young people have values, beliefs, patterns of thought, and a view of reality which is basically "frozen" in the mind. For the cult to recruit them, these patterns must be eliminated. In fact, the convert's very *identity* will be attacked and his reality disoriented so that he ceases to critically evaluate information. He just accepts it.

Step 2 is "changing." Once the victim is disarmed, with his preconceptions in a state of flux, the cult moves in with its own doctrines and view of reality, with the goal of giving the convert a totally new psychological identity. Meetings, tapes, videos, retreats—all are used in this process.

Step 3 is "refreezing." This is the reinforcement of the new identity through service to the group and the continuation of the manipulation that pulled in the victim at the beginning.

Knowing this process has taken place, your task will be to "unfreeze" your child's mind, but without the use of deception, as the cult did. There are several ways to attempt this. You may ask to attend group meetings with your child to learn more. Then, once you are a potential "recruit," you can ask the critical mind-opening questions that *he* should have asked but never did.

You may also attempt to subtly remind him of his life before he joined the cult—all the people he helped, the good things he did, the way God blessed his life. Was it *all* just a satanic delusion? Without it seeming to be a conspiracy, contact by other friends and family members can help. By all these methods, the goal is to get the cultist to look at reality from different directions.

This is the time when you may most effectively come in with doctrinal refutations and false prophecies. Even if he is resistant at this point, you can assert, "Put yourself in my shoes. Wouldn't this look a little suspicious?"

Offer the True Alternative

Finally, offer an alternative. Show him how his idealism or hurt can *truly* be met only by Jesus Christ, not some organization. Again, different circumstances and family histories may dictate different combinations of methods. Instant success is rare; many times it can take years for the seeds you plant to sprout up.

But remember that while the cults are sucking in millions, they are a revolving door: Millions are also leaving. Walter Davis, Douglas Wiskow, Steven Hassan, Steve Kemperman, and Nancy Johnson all escaped from the cults and were restored to their families. Thousands of other parents are also seeing their children come out from under the spell of the cults each year.

Your love, communication, and prayers can be very effective weapons in your warfare to free your child from a cult. Don't give up; keep persevering!

RESOURCES

Books:
> *Answers to the Cultist at Your Door*, by Robert and Gretchen Passantino
> *Witnesses of Jehovah*, by Leonard and Marjorie Chretien
> *The God Makers*, by Ed Decker and Dave Hunt
> *Another Gospel*, by Ruth Tucker
> *What You Should Know About Jehovah's Witnesses*, by Lorri MacGregor

Videos:
> *Witnesses of Jehovah* (Jeremiah Films)
> *The God Makers* (Jeremiah Films)
> *Witness at Your Door* (Jeremiah Films)
> *The Mormon Dilemma* (Jeremiah Films)

Organizations:
> See "Further Help" at back of book

CHAPTER THIRTEEN

Training for a New World Order

The philosophy of the classroom in one generation will become the philosophy of government in the next.

—Abraham Lincoln

Who rules the youth, rules the future.
—Adolph Hitler

If a foreign power wanted to conquer America, they wouldn't have to fire a shot. They could simply win the young. This is why the future freedom of our nation—and its children—is today under the most severe attack ever launched.

You won't read about it in the headlines, and the opponent is not a foreign invader. Instead, the enemies of our Constitution are a network of American elites who have forsaken the fundamental ideals of our founders and instead embraced socialism, big government, and one-world unification. Their attack is not with armies, tanks, and missiles, but with seductive words and ideas aimed directly at the minds or our youth.

To see the fury of this enemy, consider this opinion from a leading educator, Dr. Chester Pierce of Harvard University, given to a convention of several thousand teachers:

> Every child in America who enters school with an allegiance toward our elected officials, toward our founding fathers, toward our institutions, toward the preservation of this form of government...all of this proves the children are sick, because the truly well individual is one who has rejected all of those things and is what I would call the true international child.[1]

The agenda of educators such as Dr. Pierce becomes doubly frightening when you consider that it is mirrored by the powerful field of news and entertainment. MTV, the network watched most by children, recently started a news bureau which, according to one observer, tells kids that "conservatives are evil, abortion is acceptable and religion should be dismissed."[2] The vice-president for news at MTV confirms, "We'll do anything [we] feel passionately about....I am a liberal; most of our staff is liberal."[3]

With such people pulling the strings, the political manipulation of America's youth is taking place in three major steps. The aims are twofold: *control* and *indoctrination*. And the end result will be conquest, just as if foreign tanks had rolled into every town, and an enemy had replaced our officials with their own anti-American puppets.

Giving Parents the Pink Slip

No one likes to be fired. But if you're an average American parent, chances are you're about to be. Of course, your children will remain with you. You will continue to feed and clothe them, and pay most of the bills. But it will not be *you* who is molding them. Someone else will have invisibly but powerfully replaced you.

When the public school system began in the United States in the early 1800's, there were warnings that one day it could become a recruiting tool for partisan politics—or worse. Yet the system was accepted with the general understanding that schools would operate under the doctrine of *in loco parentis*. What is *in loco parentis*? This simply meant that schools were extensions of the home—representatives acting on behalf of parents just as would a nanny or private tutor. But today the concept of *in loco parentis* has been demolished, and the worst nightmares of the early dissenters have sprung to life.

Parents' rights began to crumble as the philosophy of John Dewey and other humanists took over education in the mid-to-late 1900's. Dewey saw education not as a way to teach skills to individuals, but as a way to "socialize" groups and alter political values. Individual rights were secondary to the raw power of those who knew "what was best" for society. By the mid-1980's, noted attorney John Whitehead could write:

> ...the public school no longer represents the parent, but is an independent institution that represents the interests of the state. It logically follows, then, that when children are under the authority of public school officials, they are not under the authority of parents.[4]

In other words, when the kids are in school, the government considers itself their legal guardian!

For parents in the 1990's, this is especially bad news. Why? One element of the government's "America 2000" education reform plan is to put kids in school "from cradle to career." A suggested pilot project in St. Louis calls for schooling 16 hours a day, 7 days a week, 52 weeks a year. In 1991 U.S. Secretary of Education Lamar Alexander called for formal education to begin at three *months* of age! The issue is *legal control*, and the state is looking for more of it over the lives of your children.

No more sinister example could be found than the "Parents As Teachers" (PAT) program, which by 1991 was in 40 states. At first glance the idea sounds great. At an early age, a state-certified "parent educator" is assigned to your child to help you do a good job raising your kids, help which many parents truly need. But there's a catch: The parent educator bonds with your family through home or school visits. She offers help. She monitors progress.

And, she files reports.

As one former U.S. Health Department consultant put it, "Both parents are [periodically] evaluated.... The child is given a personal computer code number by which he can be tracked the rest of his life. There are twelve computer code definitions which label a child 'at risk.' Since the expectation is that every child will be found 'mentally ill,' there is *no code* for normal."

Like many observers, this consultant warns that PAT "will result in state control of children and reduce parents to the status of breeders and supervised custodians."[5] From day one, the government will have a hook in the child, and a sword—the threat of being labeled "unfit"—hanging over the heads of his parents.

The Trap of Mind Control

The chilling reality of how we're losing our children to the state is seen in recent developments such as these.

The use of psychotherapy in schools. This follows the assumption by prominent educators such as Dr. Pierce that normal children are "sick," and must be politically reprogrammed through therapy courses. Such courses probe into the most intimate areas of a child's life where only parents, ministers, or parentally approved psychologists were once permitted. Although largely concealed from parents, this mindset is not even seriously questioned among the upper and middle ranks of the educational establishment.

Classroom criticism of parents. Children are often egged on to doubt their parents' morality, beliefs, and authority. One question discussed by a class of third-graders was "How many of you ever wanted to beat your parents up?"[6] As in most values-free classes, the teacher is prohibited from endorsing any answer as right or wrong.

Teachers as agents of indoctrination. Another wedge between parents and children is seen in the indoctrination of teachers, which the U.S. Department of Education has labeled "change agents." *Change agents?* What is a classroom "change agent"? According to federally endorsed manuals, teachers are to be programmed to affect changes in the *moral and political values* of children. Rather than making sure pupils learn their ABC's, today's teacher is trained to play the role of "advocate-organizer-agitator" in order to conform children to "group values."[7]

Using tests to program values. Perhaps the most alarming, yet little-noted, area of invasion is assessment testing. These tests are given nationwide, often without parental notification, and often labeled as "skills achievement" tests.

Without warning, little Jimmy may be given a test which is laced with subtle and sometimes not-so-subtle queries *not about aptitude, but attitude.* Little Jimmy is forced to answer questions revealing his thoughts on sex, politics, family life, religion, and how he responds to peer pressure. The combined answers supposedly determine whether Jimmy is "deficient," what it will take to "correct" the "deficient" values, and what special courses should be used to crack his so-called "threshold" of resistance to change! Testifying before Congress, one teacher from Michigan stated:

> Students are all treated as in need or having problems. Children are being pretested, then subjected to ... values program[s] as treatment....

> No parent has ever been notified or allowed to see the materials.... The children have even been promised that their parents won't be allowed to see their answers, "so be honest."[8]

And where do little Jimmy's test results go? All answers are stored in huge computers, where Jimmy has a file made just for him—one that will be there whenever needed.

Painting America Red

Now that the state has claimed your child and installed an elaborate set of controls to enforce its "rights," what are its aims?

First you should ask, "Who is in control?" Those who dominate the system include government administrators, teacher unions, teacher colleges, educational course designers, and powerful funding foundations. All honeycomb the educational industry. The President of the United States is at the top of the pyramid and the teachers at the bottom are servants of the rest.

Exactly who are "the rest"? One is the National Education Association. The NEA is a teachers' union, and the dominant force in education in America today. In 1976, as a response to the American Bicentennial, the NEA openly endorsed centralized government, attacked capitalism, advocated putting government interests over individual rights, and urged global unification.[9] More recently, it has officially endorsed homosexuality and abortion-on-demand.

If your child is in public school, the chances are virtually certain that his teacher, all the teachers at his school, the school principal, and the administrators controlling your district and state are members of the NEA.

Under the influence of groups like the NEA, students in the school systems are deluged by attacks on the free-market system, praise for socialism, and ringing endorsements of environmentalism and one-world government. Facts about the Founding Fathers and the principles behind the Constitution are either ignored or cut to fit the liberal fashion of the day.

The most dangerous weapons have been in school textbooks and in-class curricula. Extensive research reveals hundreds of instances such as the following:

- A high school text which reads, "In China, Marxism turns the people toward a future of unlimited promise, an escalator to the stars."[10]

- Praise for figures such as Fidel Castro, and criticism for those such as Ronald Reagan.

- A history text which reads, "No nation on earth is guilty of practices more shocking and bloody than is the United States at this very hour." Unfortunately, it's not referring to abortion.[11]

And don't expect the fall of Communism to change the drift of the propaganda. In universities and liberal conclaves like the NEA we're hearing the old saw that at least under socialism, everyone was guaranteed a job, health care, etc. History has been rewritten once in textbooks, and is continuing to be.

The lesson being taught about politics and economics is reinforced in entertainment and the news media. Extensive research has shown that TV and films overwhelmingly portray businessmen as greedy villains, and almost never as honest, hardworking taxpayers meeting a payroll. Conservatives are shown to be unrealistic, backward, and shallow. Surveys of TV executives reveal incredibly liberal biases and, more importantly, a willingness to use their clout to carry *their* message to American children.

Painting America Dead

Pretend you are a ninth-grader. You take a seat in your science class, and are surprised to learn that today you are to watch a silent film. Charlie Chaplin? Not quite. You sit quietly as the lights are lowered, you hear the switch of the video player turned on, and you lift your eyes to a large screen to watch a film described by one observer as follows:

> It opened with an idyllic, rustic landscape—birds singing in the trees, mother ducks leading their young on a pleasant excursion down a creek, rabbits scampering over the ground. The scene oozed with fresh air, sunshine, and peace.
>
> Suddenly an immense tractor-bulldozer appeared. The camera zoomed in on the word "AMERICAN" emblazoned on the side...and it started overturning everything in its path. Shrubs and grass were torn apart. Exhaust filled the air.
>
> One man jumped out of the front seat and went to the embankment to drain the creek

where the ducklings had been following their mother. Another man brought over a can of gasoline, poured it over portions of the surrounding area and ignited it. Flames leaped into the air. Trees caught fire; living creatures ran for cover.

Suddenly the ducklings, who by that time had emerged from the creek, were overcome by encroaching flames and burned alive.... Nests of baby birds came crashing to the ground, and the camera zoomed in on what was left. In a final close-up, the tractor-bulldozer was shown plowing under the remains of the nest, the ducklings, and the bird eggs.

As the scene receded from the screen, this sentence flashed: "Man cannot foresee or forestall. He will end up destroying the earth."[12]

The film is the widely circulated "Cry of the Marsh." It is designed to jar youngsters into opening their minds for what often comes next—a group exercise called "Who Shall Populate the Planet?" In this session, students are forced to decide what kind of individuals will best fit into an environmentally safe, one-world Utopia. They will also decide *who will not fit in.*

What are our children getting here? It's nothing less than one of the "global education" programs that began saturating schools in the 1980's, drawing angry but futile criticism from the few conservatives in the U. S. Department of Education. For two decades the one-world vision has been part of teacher's training in educational colleges. One teacher's education textbook makes this statement:

Allegiance to a nation is the biggest stumbling block to the creation of international

government. National boundaries and the
concept of sovereignty must be abolished. The
quickest way to do this is to condition the
young...[13]

Perhaps this explains the lessons on "writing a one-
world constitution"[14] or the civics text which sings the
praises of those who believe "that only with a world
government is there a chance of saving mankind."[15]

To cap things off, while little Jimmy is drilled in the
evils of the United States and its capitalist tyrants, he
and little Susie are offered the alternative of "global
citizenship," one of the newest fads in social studies. It's
clear that when the New World Order finally comes, the
new parents of what were once our kids want to make
sure their adopted children are ready.

The Second American Revolution

Since 1776, American freedom has been won by soldiers on battlefields. But in the 1990's and beyond, it
will be won by parents protecting their children from
control and indoctrination. Yet the battle is no less real,
and the stakes no less immense.

Unfortunately, it will not be another quick Desert
Storm. This conflict will be more like Vietnam. It will be
a guerilla war fought in three territories: 1) in your own
mind and heart, as you decide whether your children's
and nation's future is worth realigning your time and
priorities; 2) in your child's mind and heart; and 3) in the
jungles of family living rooms, schoolrooms, school
board meetings, and television studios.

If you're a parent, you're one of the frontline soldiers
assigned to battle out victories wherever you can. But
with the right knowledge and a little guts, the future
can be yours.

Reclaiming Parenthood

The first and most essential step is to learn what it means to be a parent. Most parents today, even caring ones, are tragically ignorant.

Child psychologist David Elkind, writing in a magazine for school administrators, with a sad degree of truth contends that many parents today are convinced that home is "a prison" and children are "economic liabilities." He states that—

> childrearing is often looked upon as a recreational activity and thus ranks low on postmodern parents' priority lists.[16]

Instead of criticizing this attitude, Elkind goes on to urge the school administrators to exploit the situation by seizing further control of other people's children.

How far we have fallen!

Starkly contrasting to today's concept, the Bible outlines the forgotten origins and responsibilities for parenting. If these were implemented, there would be little danger of any parent being "fired" by the state. In fact, the Bible reveals that parents have not so much been fired as they have resigned.

Origins. The Bible teaches that the family is the first institution created by God, and that parents are directly responsible to God for their children. If something goes wrong, the parents, not the state, are primarily accountable.

Provision and protection. The first responsibility of parents is *provision* for their children. The second duty is *protection.* Few modern parents would argue with these, yet they are very willing to let the government assume such chores without considering the price. The fact is that all the "free" services provided by day care, schools, and agencies mean that these institutions spend more and more time with your child, teaching your child more and more of *their* values. *The services aren't free at all!* The price you may pay is a portion of your child's soul.

The solution? First, *don't accept services you can provide on your own.* Make the distinction between those services your child *needs* to have provided by an outside institution and those you could provide yourself, such as meals, time, companionship, communication, and some forms of recreation. Don't get caught using government institutions as babysitters. Radical parental involvement is a revolutionary idea, but a sorely needed one. The question is, What are you willing to sacrifice for children free from state control and indoctrination?

Second, *have the right mindset.* Just because your child may get certain services through school, the child is still yours. Never apologize to a bureaucrat for calling the shots in your child's life.

Third: *Correction, discipline, training, education.* John Whitehead notes:

> The Bible lists several options for education, but none of them replace or overrule the parents. The parents are the first and main teachers. They are also responsible to supervise any outside instruction the children may receive....In fact, the family is where the child first learns religion, government (hopefully, self-government), and a wide range of subjects currently thought to be the sole province of the state schools.[17]

But can the educational function be delegated to an outside institution? According to both the Old and New Testaments, yes. But to whom is it delegated? In the Old Testament, to the priests, and in the New Testament, to the church. *Never is a state school mentioned.* Of course, public education isn't prohibited, but any delegation you allow must be in accordance with Scripture. And if your child's school is in any way teaching things that contradict the teachings of the child's Creator, then you—the steward chosen by the Creator—are *required* to step in and confront the situation by asserting your responsibility. This means:

1) You have the responsibility to prepare your child morally and intellectually to withstand school indoctrination.

2) You have the right and responsibility to contradict the teachers, and to educate your children correctly at every point where the school is contrary to the Bible.

3) You have the right and responsibility to inspect all school material and lessons.

4) You have the legal right to withdraw your child from any activity you deem improper, including tests intended to alter values or probe personality, religion, or political views. (See the sample letter in the Appendix.)

Challenge When You Must

Things got so bad for Anita Hoge of Pennsylvania and her son Garrett that she had him copy questions given during values-clarification testing and phone her from school during any "surprise" attitude tests. When she used these as ammunition to challenge the school, she was ridiculed by the principal and various officials. But in the end she got her son exempted (for which he was quite grateful) and in the process opened an investigation which has now helped thousands of parents and children.

As with Mrs. Hoge, a likely response of the school to the last three actions will be to tell you that you have no rights. Don't believe it. The answer is to contact a Christian attorney proficient in this field and threaten the school. They *will* back down. Indeed, in case after case they are doing so.

Always remember that children are not only a gift from God but also a *responsibility*. They do not belong to the government, and should not be left to TV or peers to raise, either. Monitor and restrict your children's viewing. As they grow, watch TV with them, and interpret for them the meaning of the issues and the biases implanted in the media. When you help them sharpen their discernment you are helping them grow into free, mature adults and citizens.

You are responsible, and rearranging your lifestyle and priorities might be necessary to fulfill your *obligation*. One man recently told me he considers his children to be "on loan" from above. That's a perspective that you need to have.

Know Your Civics

The first part of the political seduction of our children is *control*. If you meet that threat the second part remains: *political indoctrination*. The problem is that children have no built-in knowledge of the principles of free government or American history. They believe what they're taught in schools, movies, TV, and other sources. The solution, then, is to discover these principles yourself, and then teach them to your children starting at the earliest practical age.

What will you teach them? First, a correct view of government and economics depends on a correct view of human nature. Humans run governments. Humans buy and sell. So tell your child about humans.

Tell them that humans are two things. First, they are made in the image of God. Like God, they are capable of great creativity and beauty. As God's image-bearer, each individual is also given what our Declaration of Independence calls "inalienable rights." Yet humans are also depraved, sinful, and in need of restraint. They cannot be trusted with too much power. As one Founding Father said, "If men were angels, no government would be necessary."

The Wisdom of the Founders

Our Constitution sprang from this view of man. The Founders invented a system which tapped into the productive and creative power of the individual, while at the same time restraining depravity by limiting the potential for unchecked power. They put together an intricate system of checks and balances. The key was an effective, but limited, government. They knew that if people had access to a centralized power, it would serve as a lightning rod for their evil nature and lust for power. The result was our Constitution, which balanced power between three separate federal branches, and between the federal and state governments. With the proper understanding of human nature, government is so simple that even a child can comprehend it. And he will—but only if you tell him.

Free-market capitalism works somewhat the same way. Competition harnesses God-given creativity and produces general good. Government's limited economic role is to make sure that rules of fair trade are kept and that cheating is punished. Limited government keeps the evil in mankind from using the government to dominate everyone else. The key is seeing man's basic sinful nature, yet not ignoring his God-given individual dignity, rights, and creativity.

Why then is socialism bad? Think about it. In a socialist system the government owns everything and has all the power. Private competition is nonexistent, and the incentive to produce goods and services inexpensively and efficiently dies. From a biblical viewpoint, man's God-given individual rights and dignity are unprotected, his creativity and productivity are smothered, and his evil is unrestrained because the leaders are handed unchecked governmental power.

One-world globalism also suffers from the same shortsightedness. Like socialism, it underestimates the power of sin and jeopardizes the dignity of God's image in the individual. One-world schemes are a modern attempt to rebuild the Tower of Babel, and will only bring on the miseries of dictatorship.

Finally, you will need to counter the factual errors and propaganda pervading your child's school lessons and entertainment. Search out truly good history books and read them to your children. Christian home school catalogs are a good source of excellent texts. Let your children know about the attempts to brainwash them, and help them find ways to thwart the system. With prayer and commitment you'll find yourself learning, having fun, and promoting the freedom and righteousness which our forefathers passed on to the care of our generation.

Expose the Takeover

The process of control and indoctrination is gradual, and not always easy to spot, because it is a well-formulated strategy that allows years to be spent in silently preparing a coming generation for political harvest.

That's why you'll have to study and get your facts straight if you want to expose the scheme to other parents, or challenge it at an official level. I recommend some of the books in the *Further Help* section. The legality of many of the tests and courses used by educators to pry away control of parents is currently under question, and *national* networking is essential to compiling our case.

Once you have done your research, network with other parents locally and follow the steps for school interaction recommended in Chapter 3. It will take guts, but ever since Lexington and Concord, Valley Forge and Bunker Hill, American fathers and mothers have been willing to pay such a high price for freedom!

RESOURCES

Books:

> *Educating for a New World Order*, by B.K. Eakman
> *Parents Rights*, by John Whitehead
> *Students' Legal Rights in the Public Schools*, by J. W.
> Brinkley (booklet; to order, call International
> Christian Media at 1-800-347-5151)

Organizations:

> See "Further Help" at back of book

Your Kids at God's Funeral

[We] consider the religious forms and ideas of our fathers no longer adequate....No deity will save us; we must save ourselves.
    —Humanist Manifesto II, 1973

On humanist assumptions, life leads to nothing, and every pretence that it does not is a deceit.
    — Humanist scholar
    H.J. Blackham

The prayer I'll never forget was uttered by a woman I'll never know. I heard it several years ago while sitting in the office of a pastor friend of mine.

He had installed a public dial-a-prayer line with a unique twist: After a brief message and a prayer, the caller could talk into the machine up to several minutes. The church staff would then listen to the tape and pray for the needs of the callers.

We had listened to some anguished people pour out their hearts on that tape. But nothing compared to the prayer of what sounded like a middle-aged woman who ended five minutes of private turmoil with these words: "Oh, God... Oh, God, please be there. Is someone there? Please, please let someone be there."

Her plea haunted me for days. Is "Someone" there?

That's a question that children all around us are asking today. It is one that has tormented an increasing number of people in the last hundred years of our society, but it is an especially crucial question for parents in the 1990's. That's because the answer given by too many authority figures, and now the children themselves, is a resounding *no*.

Breakdown of Secular Humanism

You've probably heard the term "secular humanism" before. But if you're like most Christian parents, you may never have understood what it meant or been aware of its surprising influence over your child's behavior. Secular humanism is made of two components:

"Secular"... means that it excludes the concept of God or the supernatural. It either denies the existence of God or claims He is not relevant to day-to-day life and shouldn't be "preached at" anybody.

"Humanism"... means that man is the center of the universe, not God. Man is the be-all and end-all, his own beginning and end, his own alpha and omega. Whether referring to the individual or society as a whole, man is in the driver's seat, not God.

Secular humanism began as an optimistic philosophy which sought to help man fulfill his own potential by dethroning the "mythical" God of Christianity. It literally swept through society in the 1900's gaining control of key centers of intellectual power, especially education, literature, and the arts.

But unable to supply society with a vision of ultimate meaning or purpose, and saddled with a blindness to human sin, secular humanism has degenerated into a combination of prideful selfishness and hopeless despair—chaotic forces that are destroying a whole generation of children. In fact, almost all the social cesspools covered in the second section of this book can be traced back to this single poisonous stream.

Rescuing your child from the confused backwaters of secular humanism will depend on how well you yourself grasp its essential premises. It's too easy to come off looking like the caricature of the "know-nothing" Christian portrayed by the media. The philosophy of secular humanism presents a serious challenge, and one that you must take seriously if you hope to compete against it in the battle for your children.

Planting the Seeds of Doubt

Violence. Ignorance. Suicide. Drugs. Sex. Self-destruction. When you peel back the horrors that increasingly tend to characterize our children, you'll find near the center a layer of despair. And when you look underneath that despair, you'll find the loneliness of life without God.

"Life," says the lyrics to one popular rock song, "is just like beating a dead horse." Another popular song follows a series of violence-glorifying lyrics with the claim that "life ain't nothing but a piece of existence." Where does this deathly vision of life come from?

The gnawing doubt that God exists, or that He is relevant or knowable, has slowly been eating its way to the surface of our society since the mid-1800's. Today it is an open scandal. If God exists, He doesn't give a rip about man, and He certainly can't be relied upon. At best He is being purposely coy and doesn't intend to be pushed on anyone. The reality, they believe, is that He probably isn't there at all.

Take the famous series on science, *Cosmos*, shown widely on the Public Broadcasting System. Created by noted author, scientist, and pop philosopher Carl Sagan, it is now offered in video form in high schools throughout the nation. The book version is found in countless school libraries. What are Sagan's views about the ultimate nature of man and God? He begins the series by stating that the cosmos "is all that is or ever was or ever will be."[1] No God. Only matter and energy dancing in endless combinations. Sagan ends with the pronouncement that humans are nothing but "starstuff"—one-dimensional conglomerations of atoms which originated in the stars, with no soul or spirit which interacts with the body. Religious beliefs are presented as quaint relics of the past which presumably should be quarantined to the "literature" section of the library.

Two Kinds of Attacks

Cosmos follows the lead of science courses which teach theories such as evolution that contradict the Bible and exclude any scientific evidence that supports the biblical view. It is accusation by omission. While never mentioning a "religious" word, it says *everything* to your child about religious belief. The deletion of "God's side" of the evidence, and the refusal to acknowledge His role in the crucial events of creation and life, has literally shaped the minds of a generation of pupils.

Sometimes the attack is overt, but often it can be quite subtle. Mel and Norma Gabler cite the following typical example of a question in a grade-school values-clarification lesson which calls into question the basic beliefs of Christianity:

> Here's an exercise that's presented above a half-page picture of Jacqueline Kennedy and her daughter, Caroline, kneeling before the

casket of assassinated President John F. Kennedy:

There are no right or wrong answers to these questions. Choose the answers that seem best for you.

(1) Is there life after death?
   Strongly believe there is
   Might be
   Not sure
   Probably not
   Sure there is not[2]

This was part of an innocent-sounding book, *Let's Talk About Health*, and illustrates once more why you need to examine *every* book your child is given!

Take note that while this is not an outright denial of God's existence, it portrays the issue as very debatable at best. Most importantly, it does so in the middle of a total educational context that *does* attack the existence of God. Other areas of instruction are not at all hesitant in expressing what children should think about this question. Subtle exercises like this one plant seeds of doubt. Then, in the very same educational setting, other messages cause the seed to blossom.

Reaping the Bitter Harvest

No prayer was offered at the 1990 graduation ceremony at Nathan Bishop Middle School. For many years, graduation ceremonies at public schools all across the United States have included an invocation—a short prayer—asking God's blessing upon all those venturing on to the next leg of life's journey. And that's the way it was at Nathan Bishop, in Providence, Rhode Island.

That is, until 1990. A federal district court had ruled that the previous year's graduation had violated the U.S. Constitution by allowing the recitation of a prayer by a Jewish Rabbi, Leslie Gutterman, who had the audacity to invoke the name of God within earshot of students who might have been contaminated by such language.

Even though the First Amendment to the U.S. Constitution guarantees freedom of religious expression in public places and prohibits its silencing, the court declared that "God has been ruled out of public education as an instrument of inspiration and consolation."[3]

This was just one more misapplication of the doctrine of "separation of church and state," a phrase which never appears in the Constitution and which was coined by Thomas Jefferson in his argument against a government-sponsored church, *and not against private religious beliefs expressed in public schools.* This abuse of the "separation of church and state" principle by secular humanists is most ironic. Secular humanism (which the law considers to be a religion) has in practice become the only permissible faith of the government, thereby forcing out Christianity and all other religions as humanism is crammed down the throats of schoolchildren by the millions.

Following the Connecticut ruling, states in other parts of the nation began working to bar prayers from school graduation ceremonies, erasing over two century's worth of tradition. Yet the Rhode Island case is only a recent symptom of a concerted attack on religion (especially the conservative Jewish and Christian faiths), an attack that has proceeded for years with the goal of rinsing clean future generations of the "backward" notion of a biblical God.

If only a quick, interdenominational prayer at a once-a-year ceremony were the issue, the alarm felt by Christian parents might not be so great. However, much more is at stake if instances like that at Providence succeed in wiping the Judeo-Christian religion off the

educational map, because inside the classroom the
attacks become even more vicious and influential.

Exit Jesus Christ, Enter Barbra Streisand

Consider the case of Charity Licharwitz. Charity
was a third-grader at Winston Elementary School in
Miami, Florida, who was given the assignment of writing a biography of any famous historical figure of her
choice and presenting it to the class. Her choice was
Jesus Christ, the founder of the Christian religion.

But when Charity informed the teacher of her decision, she was told that Jesus would be appropriate in
Sunday school but totally *inappropriate* in her public
school classroom. The teacher, who reportedly spoke in a
tone that had the other students giggling and snicker-
ing, told Charity that the report had to be based "on a
real person." If she wanted to do Jesus, she would have to
take a failing grade. In the end, Charity did her report
on Barbra Streisand.[4]

If students can't stand up to the educational establishment over the issue of God, can a teacher? Ask
Mission Viejo, California, science teacher John Peloza,
runner-up Science Teacher of the Year, who was fired
from his seven-year high-school position for teaching
the scientific evidence for intelligent design of the universe alongside the evolutionists' view of a random,
Godless creation.

Fortunately, this is not the final word in all three of
these cases: All are being litigated, one at the Supreme
Court level. Yet they are only the tip of an iceberg.
Secular humanism spreads out its tentacles not only in
the schools but on TV and movies, and in zoos and
museums, where literature subtly undermines the
Bible's perspective on nature and suppresses the sup-
porting evidence. As the Bible reveals in Romans 1,
mankind desires to serve the creation while denying the

204 Marlin Maddoux

obvious evidence for the Creator. This is a trap that will demand your ingenuity to keep your children from falling prey to it.

The Hidden Message of Humanism

The humanists put their ideals into written "doctrinal statements" twice: first in 1933, then again in 1973 to add, among other things, a more strongly atheistic tone. The documents are the Humanist Manifestos I and II. Prominent leaders in education, science, the arts, and government signed the papers. They have been a blueprint for a half-century of grief caused the American people. Beginning with the denial of God, the documents call for elimination of nations, expansion of irreligious public schools, abolition of virtually all sexual standards, socialist economics, gradual death of churches, and reliance on self rather than the "fables" of Christian belief.

But the embarrassing problem for the secular humanists is that their attempt to build a Utopia without God has boomeranged, with hideous consequences for our children.

If the spirit of death pervades our children's culture it is because too many of them perceive life as simply another form of death. It's the logical conclusion—and children are very logical—of the worldview of secular humanism. Today, like fallen Communism, that secular hope is a cruel joke upon those caught in its undertow.

The Bible and most other religions say that God gave man life. Take away God and you've taken away the uniqueness of life. Man becomes a sophisticated rock, a well-organized collection of dust placed here by random evolutionary chance and who will ultimately be forgotten by a cold, dark universe. Supreme Court Justice Oliver Wendell Holmes was one of the leading forces for weaving secular humanism into the fabric of our society. He stated:

> I see no reason for attributing to man a signifi-
> cance different in kind from that which be-
> longs to a baboon or a grain of sand....I
> believe that our personality is a cosmic gan-
> glion, just as when certain rays meet and
> cross...[5]

The late Dr. Jacob Bronowski, host of the powerfully influential television series *The Ascent of Man* (another video shown in colleges and public schools), said, "Man is part of nature, in the same sense that a stone is, or a cactus, or a camel."

Your Kids at Their Own Funeral

Carl Sagan may try to glamorize the predicament of secular humanism by pronouncing that we are all "star-stuff," but filmmaker Woody Allen is more perceptive about the implications of this, implications which are not lost on our kids.

In an article in *Esquire* magazine he wrote: "The fundamental thing behind *all* motivation and *all* activity is the constant struggle against annihilation and against death. It's absolutely stupefying in its terror, and renders anyone's accomplishments meaningless."[6] Humanist H. J. Blackham admits:

> On humanist assumptions, life leads to noth-
> ing, and every pretence that it does not is a
> deceit. If there is a bridge over a gorge which
> spans only half the distance and ends in mid-
> air, and if the bridge is crowded with human
> beings pressing on, one after the other they
> fall into the abyss. The bridge leads nowhere,
> and those who are pressing forward to cross it
> are going nowhere....Such a situation is a
> model of futility.[7]

But this is many of our children's view of the universe. No matter what candy coating the secularists apply, the kids are smart enough to see through it to the grim reality. This is a view which admits no God and puts man in the driver's seat of his own destiny. The problem is that without God there is nowhere to drive.

What does this do to little Johnny as he trudges home from school listening to his Walkman with a rock band singing to him that life is nothing but "beating a dead horse"? One, it scares him. Two, it can make him very depressed. Three, it takes away all ultimate boundaries for right and wrong, all transcendent standards. Where are moral laws if there is no Lawgiver? And four, it focuses his attention on maximizing sensual pleasure to make life meaningful. Experience becomes everything—sex, money, drugs, career, materialism, religion, food, television, thrills, amusement, power. Each to his own experience! Each one's experience is used to wall out the reality of death and meaninglessness—except for those suicidal children for whom death *is* the chosen experience.

The truth is stark and simple: The "death" of God has meant the death of man. The denial of deity means the denial of human dignity and worth. Using their incredibly insightful "baloney antennas," children have seen straight through the secularists' phony optimism with brutal frankness. The pity of it is that they are now logically acting out the pessimistic worldview they have been given.

Hope and Help in a Godless Society

Today's generation of American children is the first to live through such a significant shift. We have gone from a society where Christianity still pervaded the major institutions (and gave some ultimate religious hope to the basic questions of life, death, and meaning) to a society where Christian thinking has been locked in a corral, and with it all hope.

How do we put hope back into our children's world? The first step is to treat them as if God existed, and let the unspoken message do its work. That by itself won't be enough, but it will be the crucial beginning of the battle.

How does that happen? The place to begin is with the Golden Rule. Jesus said, "Love your neighbor as yourself.... Love your enemies, and pray for those who persecute you." Do your children see the reality of God's transforming life in your behavior? When you're cut off on the freeway, do they see you curse the offender? Do they see merely "a form of godliness without the power" in your treatment of them and others? Do you take time for them, and sacrifice your time to make people a priority in your life? Or do you project a reverence for material possessions and human adulation, and pass that worldview on to your kids? Do you attend a church where Christian enthusiasm and sacrificial caring are absent?

The wrong answers to these questions open the gateways for secular humanism to creep into your children's lives. These are broken gates that need to be mended to keep the enemy out.

The next challenge posed to Christian parents was well stated by professor Edmund Leach of Cambridge University, a leading secular humanist:

> Our idea of God is a product of history. What I now believe about the supernatural is derived from what I was taught by my parents, and what they taught me was derived from what they were taught, and so on. But such beliefs are justified by faith alone, never by reason, and the true believer is expected to go on reaffirming his faith in the same verbal formula

even if the passage of history and the growth
of scientific knowledge should have turned the
words into plain nonsense.[8]

Does your son or daughter believe Christianity just
because you do? Is their belief in God just a "verbal
formula"?

Sooner or later they must come to their own conclusions about God. However, your input will be a key in
this process, and this means that you must learn to
defend your faith and convey that defense to your children. They must see the reality of the Bible in your life,
but they also must be helped to think it through intellectually, to know that "the passage of history and the
growth of scientific knowledge" do not, in fact, render
the literal truth of the Bible "plain nonsense."

Picking Secularism Apart

The first place to attack the humanist worldview is
the issue of "randomness versus design." The classroom
is anywhere you want it to be.

This process starts simply, at an early age. Pick a
clear, friendly night and go for a drive with your little
boy or girl away from the city lights. Help them fix their
gaze upward to the array of stars. Tell them about the
vastness and beauty of the universe, and the place of
earth in that universe. Talk to them about the impos-
sibility that it could have happened by accident, with no
ultimate cause. Psalm 19 says:

> The heavens declare the glory of God; the
> skies proclaim the work of his hands. Day
> after day they pour forth speech; night after
> night they display knowledge. There is no
> speech or language where their voice is not
> heard. Their voice goes out into all the earth,
> their words to the ends of the world.

Next, point out to them the intricacy of nature, especially the human body. Then show them the complex of metal, tubes, and wiring under the hood of your car. Explain to them how it works. Take the top off your PC. Open the back of a clock. Explain how the human body is vastly more complex and ordered than these things. Only a fool would say that the car, computer, or clock "just happened"! Even if it took billions of years, the odds against such a thing "just happening" are much too great. How much greater, then, are the odds against the existence of God?

Of course, this might take a bit of self-education on your part. But don't despair, because many books, tapes, and videos—produced by top-notch scholars with earned degrees from well-known universities, but who communicate at the common man's level—are available at Christian bookstores and from various ministries.

It might also interest you to know that Christians aren't the only ones skeptical of evolution. In the past several years, top secular scientists and scholars have stepped up the attack on evolution. Citing what creationists have been saying for years, these scientists site the lack of convincing fossil evidence for evolutionary transitions between species (despite misleading "finds" puffed up in the press which always turn out to be highly disputed). They also point out the insurmountable odds against all of the proposed ways that species could alter beyond certain limitations. These sources are a *must* for any junior high school to college-aged youth being exposed to evolutionist propaganda for several hours every week in the classroom.

They are also a must for *you*. After reading just one or two good books exposing the scientific fallacies of the arguments of atheism, you should be able to sit down with your child and enjoy an hour of "National Geographic" on television, explaining to him the mistaken assumptions and misinterpretations being peddled as fact. The result is that your child can become a tough-minded, confident Christian rather than a shrinking, pietistic wallflower afraid to confront his culture for Christ.

After your appeal to nature, the next point of attack is an appeal to conscience. As soon as your child is old enough to comprehend, ask him or her, "If there is no God, then why is anything right or wrong?" We all know instinctively that right and wrong exist. The only reason not to believe in God is to try to fool ourselves in order to get away with doing wrong. This is why people sin, and then try to deny God. The only explanation for it all is that God exists, and we have tried to kick Him out of our world.

Putting Feet to Your Child's Faith

The third hammer blow you can strike will be the defense of the Bible as the inspired, inerrant (without error) revelation from God. The first step is biblical literacy, but more is needed. Too many Christian youth today have no idea how the Bible has been historically transmitted to us down through the centuries, or the powerful case for its claim to be directly from God.

One of the worst mistakes you can make, both as a Christian and a parent, is to assume that this material is too boring and stuffy to learn and get excited over. The fulfillment of prophecy, the astounding coherence of themes throughout the Bible, the compilation of the Scriptures—all these and more are good places to begin learning. There are excellent books debunking the so-called biblical "contradictions" that skeptics like to toss about. It's fascinating to find out the *facts*. And by the time your child is in middle school, high school, or college, these are facts that he or she will need to have.

The final assault against secular humanism is helping your child to *apply* the Bible correctly. If the Bible is the Word of God, then every Christian child has an overwhelming advantage against the despair and hopelessness of the 1990's and beyond. But they'll need your help in applying it to the pressures they face day to day. They'll need you to help interpret it, to bring out its teachings on sex, violence, abortion, and other tension points. And they'll need your encouragement to resist the growing humiliation regularly faced by children who decide to obey God rather than men.

CHAPTER FIFTEEN

Godhood for Your Kids?

At this point the kids are more than ready. The media has done a lot of work for us.[1]
—Jack Canfield
New Age educator

They are ready to fall into the hands of almost anyone who comes along.[2]
—Tal Brooke
former New Age adherent

Rhode Island—An 11-year-old girl comes home to tell her mother about a strange new course being taught at her middle school.

While lying on their backs in the darkened room, the children are told to close their eyes and visualize stepping into a magic elevator which will take them to a special chamber. When the doors open, they see in the center of the chamber any object they wish. They can communicate with the object, and it will tell them the answers to anything they want to know.

Finally the children are told to visualize floating outside their bodies, so that they can look down and view themselves from the outside.

Meditation. Telepathy. Astral projection. All this and it's still only day one of a five-day lesson.

Seattle, Washington—An entire continent away from the Rhode Island middle school, an instructor guides a group of fourth-graders through the same type of journey—except that this lesson goes a step farther. Without parental notification or consent, the youngsters in Seattle are introduced not only to imaginary talking objects but to *actual spirit guides*—helpers who will be their personal counselors for every problem or question in life. They are also taught about a "cord of fire" that extends from their belly into infinity, through which they can use the power of their mind to influence people and change reality at will.

Many of the children begin to experience "the Babbler," a small voice speaking inside them telling them what to do. They are also reportedly asked by teachers not to say anything about this to their parents.[3]

The Tidal Wave Has Hit

These are not isolated examples of some passing fad. Instances like these, which could be multiplied by the thousands around the nation, are part of a tidal wave that is flooding schools, movies, children's cartoons, comic books, science fiction and fantasy novels, and music. It is the New Age movement, or "New Age humanism"—the successor to secular humanism, and the second wave of humanism to erode the shores of Christian belief in the United States during this century.

The New Age jumped in when secular humanism eliminated God and promised optimism but delivered only despair. Once the culture had become addicted to humanistic self-centeredness, yet weary of a universe without hope, the New Age movement offered a powerful brand of *spiritual* humanism that is now competing head-to-head with its secular forerunner. And since the despair of secular humanism hit our children hardest of all, why be surprised if it is the children who begin flocking to the false hope of the New Age?

Much has been written on the New Age in the last decade. But after all the words, many Christian parents still struggle to define, much less combat, this powerful system.

In a nutshell, the New Age movement is the blending and repackaging of key elements of Eastern religion (mainly Hinduism, paganism, and Buddhism) with terminology and concepts acceptable to people in the West, especially North America. Not all New Agers believe precisely the same thing; some are more deeply involved than others. But throughout the entire far-flung movement are five core beliefs that characterize its basic foundation.

Know these beliefs. Know how to spot them. Know why they are wrong. And most importantly, know how to explain why they are wrong to your children.

"All Is One"... Or Is It?

Serious followers of the New Age believe that what we perceive to be real is just an illusion. They contend that everything is composed of one underlying spiritual substance. This principle sets the stage for everything else they believe.

The Beatles, early pioneers of New Age evangelism of the United States, sang, "I am you and you are me and he is we and we are all together." This is the essence of "monism"—all is one.

Is it biblical? Is it even reasonable?

In contrast to New Age beliefs, the Bible teaches that the universe is a *plurality*—that God ordained *real differences and distinctions* in His creation. This is seen in the Genesis account of creation, and it is reinforced by God's assignment to Adam to give different names to the varieties of animals. Even God Himself is a trinity. In perfect alignment with this is the testimony of science, which has never found that matter and energy are reducible to one substance.

Yet this erroneous belief is the basis for much of what our children are being taught in movies, cartoons, and school curricula with New Age themes. For this reason, make sure your children understand that God made things basically distinct and different for a purpose. This important but often overlooked truth can literally chop off New Age deception at the roots.

Is Everything God?

Secular humanists believe that the universe is non-living except for random accidents such as life on earth. In contrast, New Age humanists hold that *everything* is spiritually alive. And, they reason, since all is one, since all is living, and since there is nothing other than "all," then this "all" must be God! This teaching is in fact classic Hindu pantheism (pan = all, theos = God).

Of course, the God of the New Age is usually seen as impersonal, an "it": god rather than God. It is "The Force" of the movie *Star Wars*, not the personal Holy Spirit of the Bible to whom Jesus referred with pronouns such as "He" and "Him" (John 16:7,8).

This is where you need to teach your kids to be extremely careful. A lot of pantheism is running rampant today even in circles that carry the label "Christian." One frequent snare is the argument that since the Bible teaches that God exists *everywhere* (omnipresence) He is therefore *everything*. To the uncritical mind, especially that of a child, this sounds plausible.

What would you say if your child asked you about this? How would your respond if your daughter heard it from a college instructor, read it in a high school or junior high school book, or was exposed to it in a grade-school exercise in "relaxation"? A member of my staff recounted an experience filled with instruction for adults seeking to shape the lives of young people faced with such questions.

Raising Wimps or Warriors?

He said, "My wife and I were teaching a fifth- and sixth-grade Sunday school class. We knew that the scheduled topic—God's omnipresence—was destined to hold their interest for about six seconds.

"So before the six seconds were up, I asked the class if they knew who Shirley MacLaine was. That got their attention. Then I asked if they knew what she said about God. Since her New Age movie *Out On A Limb* was headline news at that time, all the kids locked right into what I was saying.

"The first thing I said was that she believed that everything was God: the chalkboard, the chairs, their clothes, all of us. Everything is God! That got a few giggles.

"But I quickly said, 'Hey, wait! Why isn't she right?

"'Doesn't the Bible say that God's Spirit exists everywhere, and that He sees everything we do and knows every thought we think? He's in this room, He's on Mars, He sees the termites in the wood and the worms underneath the ground, so how can He *not be* everything?'

"Blank stares, with a little apprehension. I gave them a few seconds to think, then let them in on 'the radio wave illustration.'

"I said, 'Here's why Shirley MacLaine and her New Age friends are wrong, and why they hate Christianity so much. Are you ready?

"'The Bible says that God exists everywhere, but that He is not everything. How can that be? Think about a radio. To put out music, radio waves travel from an antenna many miles away, going through walls, trees, hills, and air.

"'But do those waves *become* the walls, the trees, the hills, or the air? Of course not! The two *exist* together in the same space without *being the same thing*. This is a lot like God and the universe He created. God can be *everywhere* without *being everything*.

"'Shirley MacLaine and her gang have been tricked about this because *they want to be God*! They don't want to *worship* God, they want to *be* God just as the Bible says the Devil wants to be God, and just as he tricked Eve by telling her that she could be God.

"'And now they want to trick you, too, to make you believe that you don't need Jesus. But the Bible says this is ridiculous, and whenever you hear someone telling you differently just think about what the Bible says, and about the radio waves. It just doesn't work.'"

A simple truth, and a simple illustration, yet I've talked with many young people who lacked such teaching early in life and have gone on to break their parents' hearts by naively buying into the New Age lie.

That's why whenever you teach your child the Bible, do it with an eye to the strong objections they will face in the real world. In fact, the Bible warns us to be prepared for such clever attacks, for "Satan himself masquerades as an angel of light" (2 Corinthians 11:14). Therefore, "Always be prepared to give an answer to everyone who asks you to give the reason for the hope you have" (1 Peter 3:15).

How old must a child be before this Scripture applies? With the kind of tests being pitted against kids today, it is almost never too early to start! Ask yourself: "Will the challenges and clever deceptions of spiritual enemies strengthen my child or weaken him? Will my son or daughter be the kind of tough-minded Christian so desperately needed today, or the kind spiritual wimp so typical today in our lukewarm churches?"

Are You God?

Several years ago an educational planner in Los Angeles named Beverly Galyean was granted federal funds to help pioneer the enormously influential "confluent education." One of Galyean's major premises was the following:

> Once we begin to see that we are all God, that we all have the attributes of God, then I think the whole purpose of human life is to reown the Godlikeness within us....[4]

And you thought the Supreme Court had kicked religion out of the classroom! Yet Galyean's "confluent education" (the coming together, or confluence, of the rational with the nonrational) became the model for many of today's public school curricula. Russell Chandler, religion editor for *The Los Angeles Times,* reports:

> Children in the Los Angeles City School System have been taught to imagine they are one with the sun's rays. In doing so, they are told that they are part of God, "they are one with Him."[5]

"I am God"? Because the claim seems incredible, don't think it won't be forceful. It conforms to everything the children are learning in self-esteem training. It also appeals to the spiritual void left by atheistic secular humanism. Finally, it agrees with the relativism (the rejection of universal standards of right and wrong) being taught in the values-clarification exercises dealt with elsewhere in this book.

How do you combat this claim? First, make sure your child understands that he is made in God's image, and does have worth (see the Christian Worldview Checklist in Chapter 2). This truth eliminates the craving for a false spirituality that panders to the ego.

Second, make sure your child understands that being made in God's image does not make him God, or even a part of God. While we are all "fearfully and wonderfully made" (Psalm 139:14), we are also for that very reason all the more tragically fallen due to our willful rebellion against the God who made us. We are all sinners, and we are all suffering the corruption and decay that sin has ushered into the universe (Romans 5:12,13; 8:20,21).

The New Agers will bait your child with the lie that they are divine and perfect, and need only to recognize that inner perfection. But Jesus said, "From within, out of men's hearts, come evil thoughts" (Mark 7:21). Romans 3:10,11 states, "There is no one righteous, not even one; there is no one who understands, no one who seeks God."

But merely presenting Bible doctrine won't be enough. Practical rubber-meets-the-road thinking also needs to be done. Offer some stimulating intellectual "weight-lifting" with questions like these:

> If all people are divine, doesn't that mean that *everything* they do is not evil, but good? If so, what about Hitler—was he divine? What about a murderer—is he a perfect expression of divinity?

Teach your children to press the premises of self-deity and moral relativism to their absurd conclusions. These are questions which the New Age rejection of absolute right and wrong *cannot handle*. Our children need to be schooled in these issues as they mature into believers ready to defend themselves and their faith.

Transformation... to What?

- A course to build self-esteem is scheduled to go into hundreds of schools in a major metropolitan area. Its method: A visualized journey through a rainbow to a special place where the children will meet two "helpers." These new companions will "teach... guide... listen... and counsel" the children through life.[6]

- A teacher in a school in the Midwest takes her students on a mental "flight" outside the world to a magical place where they can do anything through the power of their thoughts, and where they can meet all kinds of "weird" creatures. She tells them that this is a place where they will want to return often on their own.

- In a small town in Texas, a class of first-graders appears on the front page of the newspaper with their eyes closed, palms up, and legs crossed on the floor, listening to their teacher take them on an imaginary journey.

  When questioned, the teacher does not claim any religious origin for the position, despite the fact that it is identical to the classic Hindu "lotus" position used for meditation. And despite the fact that her instructions are strikingly similar to those found in books on meditation and hypnosis, she denies that the children are meditating.[7]

Today's New Age educational theorists have rejected the 60's notion of mysticism induced by drugs, and have turned instead to an allegedly purer form of enlightenment—*meditation.* Yet the goal—an altered state of consciousness where a person can learn the secrets of the universe and exploit his or her psychic potential—remains the same.

According to the army of New Age educators, little Johnny doesn't need God. Instead, Johnny needs to be transformed by realizing that he *is* god. Little Susie doesn't need salvation from sin and imperfection; she needs *transformation* by realizing that she is *already* perfection. Little Jimmy doesn't need to memorize multiplication tables and take more spelling lessons; he needs to tap into the universal knowledge that *already* resides in his divine mind.

The course may be called Pumsey or DUSO, or have one of the many other names for such curricula found throughout the country. It may be labeled as relaxation, esteem-building, or drug prevention. Yet in all these forms, meditation has become a key part of today's schooling. And the goal of meditation is to experience your own divinity and unity with the cosmos, realize your divine mental power, and—at advanced stages— make contact with spirit guides who will become your counselors and masters.

Transformation Trickery

You may be wondering, "How can this happen when Christian prayers are banned by law in public schools?" First, the religious content of the curriculum is often hidden from the teachers, who truly believe they are helping children in a merely nonreligious way.

Second, course designers and those teachers who *are* aware of the indoctrination that is occurring aren't about to let parents in on their motives. Jack Canfield, a prominent educational consultant and member of California's governmental commission on self-esteem, has written: "Advice: If you're teaching in a public school, don't call it meditation, call it 'centering.' Every school wants children to be relaxed, attentive, and creative, and this is what they will get."[8]

Dick Sutphen, another New-Age-oriented educational theorist, is a bit more candid:

> One of the biggest advantages we have as New
> Agers is [that] once the occult, metaphysical

and New Age terminology is removed, we have
concepts and techniques that are very acceptable to the general public. So we can change
the names and demonstrate the power. In so
doing, we can open the door to millions who
normally would not be receptive.[9]

Beverly Galyean herself apparently understood
the implications of the "spirit guides" which her taxpayer-funded programs were introducing to children.
But her advice to educators was not to let the secret out.
She stated, "Of course we don't call them that in the
public schools. We call them imaginary guides."

What's going on outside the schoolroom? New Age
doctrine being taught in class is supported by movies
and cartoons, again mostly aimed at the children. Box-
office giant George Lucas, a devotee of Zen Buddhism,
once said, "Theaters are the churches of the 80's ... and
I'm going to preach my gospel" in them. He went on to
make some of the biggest-selling movie hits for children
ever seen, including the *Star Wars* trilogy.

These immensely popular movies, which spun off
into cartoon series, books, and a line of toys, teach that
success comes through emptying the mind and tapping
into an impersonal "Force" which connects you to enormous universal power. The turning point of the first *Star
Wars* is when the hero finally shuns his rational thinking and turns inward to "The Force."

But it doesn't stop there. Steven Spielberg created
ET around a cute extraterrestrial who mouths statements that contradict the most important teachings of
Scripture with New Age dogma. Its themes are repeated
endlessly in space-age cartoons, comics, and much contemporary science fiction literature being gobbled up by
our children. Even the "Teenage Mutant Ninja Turtles"
feature a mysticism-over-matter theme.

By the way, do your kids like spacemen? Then beware. Today's extraterrestrials are hardly the innocent brand of three decades ago. A central concept of the New Age is the existence of highly evolved spirit life-forms on distant planets. That's why it's a recurring theme in hot movies like *ET* and *Cocoon*.

And whether coming from a movie "ET," a classroom "counselor," or a psychic "channeling" a spirit from beyond, the message is invariably the same: It is standard pantheism, with the extraterrestrials and spirits urging your children to take the transformational leap away from Christianity into godhood.

Gate-Crashing a Child's Mind

Often the leading edge of the New Age invasion is comprised of the various elements of the occult that are rampaging through youth culture like a wildfire. These include:

paganism (worship of   reincarnation
    nature, gods, or   tarot cards
    goddesses)   the Ouija board
witchcraft   ESP
sorcery   ghosts
astrology

Does your child bring home books or tell you of exercises involving witches, imaginary levitation, or worship of nature? Do they get regular doses of cartoons or movies where the characters perform magic rituals? If such signs of infiltration appear in a schoolbook or TV show, take action. But remember, as the child's maturity allows, you'll need to *explain* your reasons.

So just why is the occult banned by God? Simply because these are efforts at spiritual enlightenment and transformation which go outside of God's wisely chosen conduits: the Bible, and rebirth through forgiveness of sins given exclusively through Christ, the *only*

God-man. Also, all occult practices are based on Hindu-istic ideas of pantheism (all is God) and self-deification. These attempt to tap into alleged connections between your inner divine self and the world, which can be manipulated by those who have access to hidden spiri-tual secrets. Like the in-class meditation in Rhode Island and Seattle, it is an open door to deception and control by demons.

Sometimes the transformation process gets very brutal. One tactic has been to shatter and even scar the vulnerable imaginations of our children—to unsettle them so severely that, in their confusion, they will be open to spiritually hazardous sources of comfort and new organizing principles of life. Into this category fall movies and books which rivet a child's attention on the gruesome, the morbid, and the depressing.

Yet ironically, the most infamous example is not found in a theater. Instead, it is the *Impressions* book series, published by HBJ and aggressively marketed to thousands of schools, including elementary level, across the nation. Short stories, fantasy tales, and poems in the *Impressions* texts feature explicit scenes of violent death, senseless tragedy, highly personalized mental agony, and even child abuse. Just a few typical plots include the following:

- Characters helplessly watch monsters tear the heads off their parents and eat into their brains.

- Witches cook and cannibalize children.

- A virtuous prince is beaten into uncon-sciousness and finally death by giants, with no justice or redeeming plot twist.[10]

While this sort of attack bludgeons children into a fragile state of emotional disorientation, "values-free" education pries their morals away from Christian tradition and their God-given conscience. With the child emotionally unsettled or morally unhinged, the spiritual humanists are then free to inject their own New Age explanation of reality into the newly "opened" mind.

Preventing New Age Mind Control

What can a parent do to prevent this kind of spiritually deadly conversion? First, *be alert to the dangers* as described here and in other books on the subject. Here is a thumbnail sketch of when these dangers might occur:

Ages 2-4
- Cartoons conditioning children for 1) manipulation of reality using "mind power," 2) globalism, and 3) global saviors from outer space.

Ages 5-11
- Cartoons, comic books, and movies with the same themes.
- Rock music exalting the occult.
- Literature in school giving overt or implied approval to occultic themes.
- Activities in school which may disguise meditation and spiritual transformation as "relaxation," "self-esteem improvement," or "drug and violence prevention."

Ages 12-17
- Music and literature with the themes cited above.
- More New Age education.

College
- More esoteric New Age philosophy in courses and on-campus clubs and activities.
- Music, movies, and literature.

Second, *pray for your child* to be protected from deception. Pray specifically against the threats outlined here and from other sources.

Third, *give your child a biblical education* as described in this chapter—one which will stand up to deception at strategic points. But education alone isn't enough. Discipleship—the power of God's Spirit working in every area of your child's life—is necessary to avoid spiritual tampering by both human and demonic meddlers.

Fourth, *teach your child to distinguish* between legitimate uses of the imagination and those which encourage unhealthy fantasizing and spiritual error.

Fifth, after educating yourself, *educate others*. Network with other parents and organizations. Assemble your facts and educate your children's teachers and school board if necessary. They are often pawns in a sense, as much victimized as the children.

Sixth, *insist on your rights* as a parent, and withdraw your child from any courses you deem unacceptable.

New Age Globalism

A final element of New Age teaching is globalism. I have presented one-world unification in Chapter 13, but you need to be aware of the explicitly *spiritual* aspect of this threat. Secular humanists wanted a politically unified world with no religion and no God, but New Agers want a politically unified world in which all religions unite to worship the universe itself as God. Just as they seek personal transformation of your child, they also want global transformation, which many observers believe will happen through their conversion of the youth.

The environmental movement can be a gateway here. "Gaia"—the Goddess Earth—is a term seen more and more on cartoons and television series. Even portrayals of American Indians are tending to glorify their pagan religion as a viable option.

In response, you need to teach your child to distinguish between *stewardship* of creation and *pagan worship* of it. And make sure they understand the nonnegotiable points of contradiction between biblical Christianity and all other religions to combat the New Age notion that all religions worship the same God.

New Age globalism is a future-oriented religious view. After years of success, the evidence indicates that the New Age movement may have peaked in its campaign *for those who are currently adults.* However, the new target is *the next generation,* and the New Age is buying up the souls of that generation on a wholesale basis.

CHAPTER SIXTEEN

Things That Go Bump in the Night

I made a pact to Satan. In my own blood I wrote, "I renounce God, I renounce Christ. I will serve only Satan. To my friends love, to my enemies death ... hail Satan." I placed my own name at the bottom.[1]

He is close to being a textbook case. Middle-class, white, from a two-parent, second-marriage home. Creative and bright, though not always dedicated to schoolwork. Growing up in a churched family, yet hearing little more than "God talk" with no biblical substance. Caught in an unraveling society; engulfed by the rebellious drumbeat of rock music and all its cultural trappings.

When he was age 13, he began playing *Dungeons & Dragons*, which led to an interest in the occult. Researching through the *Time/Life* book series on witches, wizards, and magic, he was pulled away from his Christian roots and began to search for something more tangible.

Along with some of his friends, he started performing dark rituals. He was obsessed with the Ninja ethic and Zen Buddhism. He frequented a heavy metal teens' club, indulging in drugs and sex. His favorite movies were slasher films, along with the cult movie *The Rocky Horror Picture Show.* Alarmed to find her son reading *The Satanic Bible,* his mother took him to see her pastor. There ensued a spirited debate over the validity of the Holy Bible versus the unholy one.

To this day, the young man remembers the clergyman obliging that many events portrayed in the Bible were almost certainly myths. But, the pastor said, the ethics were good. *The young man rejoined that he would be a fool to believe in the Bible if a Christian minister admitted he did not!* The pastor recommended that the young man's mother allow her son to have his privacy.[2]

He became more enthusiastic, recruiting still others. Later he recounted:

> I became aware of the common tie binding it all together. Satan was behind D&D [*Dungeons & Dragons*] and behind Ninjitsu. Satan was everywhere ... the force behind rebellion which led to freedom and was a way to success in a society where only the strong survive and only the ruthless attain the American dream.[3]

The events which followed fell quickly: the pact with Satan, signed in his own blood. The formation of a small cult dedicated to the "elimination" of the "hypocritical Christian community." Animal sacrifices and mutilations. Visibly conjuring demons. A vow to break all of the Ten Commandments, culminating in the arbitrary slaying of a convenience store clerk, done in "a surreal, game-like euphoria."

And finally, there came the brutal murder of his parents with a .44-caliber pistol as they lay sleeping in bed. He was 16 years of age at the time.

Highway to Hell

Sean Sellers, today on death row in Colorado, is admittedly an extreme example of satanic commitment. Yet in his story lies the ingredients of seduction for tens of thousands of others in our culture. They may not fit the profile in every detail, and they may not pursue Satanism to the limit. Yet they will walk partway down the path. And to the degree they do, they will walk away from everything worthwhile and become collaborators in the purest forms of evil.

The life of Sean Sellers exhibits all four of the social factors cited by experts as causing the rise of Satanism in our society. These are:

1) A loss of faith in our society and its leaders.

2) Churches failing to exhibit the power of Christ.

3) Broken family relationships, including lack of unconditional love wedded to discipline and guidance.

4) Widespread immorality and praise of evil, including occultism in school curricula.[4]

Against this backdrop comes the "great liberator"— cosmic freedom's answer to a tyrannical Jehovah. It is the "angel of light" (2 Corinthians 11:14), offering your children a Halloween basket full of treats. With slight variations, the allure of Satan as portrayed by his vendors includes some or all of the following, depending upon the level of involvement:

• Total freedom for man's animal passions ("Do what thou wilt"), complete with free sex and drugs if desired.

• Freedom from guilt.

- Self-redemption (the Satanic Bible says, "Say unto thine own heart, 'I am mine own redeemer'").

- Raw power.

- Insight into the metaphysical mysteries of the universe.

- Future world co-domination when Satan topples God and triumphantly storms the gates of heaven.[5]

Your child will certainly bump into at least one or more of the four problem areas I mentioned. And the sad truth is that with such a glittering sales package being pushed by the other side, an emotional bruise in *any* area can be enough to pull a child under.

Three-Pronged Attack

According to law-enforcement consultants in satanic crime, Satanism in America is operated on three levels:

The *sophisticated level* encompasses the New Age movement, witchcraft, and the general occult. It reaches where hard-core Satanism cannot, achieving respectability and influence. As we saw earlier, the influence of Satanism at this level reaches millions of people, from society's power brokers to the middle-class masses.[6]

The *serious level* is explicit, "elite" Satanism. While numerically small—perhaps no more than a few thousand people—its main role is to spearhead the movement, provide highly visible leadership, set a theoretical tone, and gain legitimacy. Examples of prominent, tax-exempt groups are The Church of Satan, led by Anton LaVey, author of *The Satanic Bible*, which in 1988 outsold the Holy Bible ten to one on college campuses. Somewhat more esoteric is the Temple of Set, initiated by Dr. Michael Aquino, a university professor and army lieutenant colonel with high honors and a security clearance.

The *self-styled level* is where your child will encounter hard-core Satanism, due to its culturally camouflaged recruiting. Satanists at this level are just as committed as those at the serious level. The difference is that they are more localized, and almost always delve into criminal activity such as theft, animal sacrifice, extortion, and violence.

The self-styled Satanist can be a lonely boy or girl in his or her room chanting to Satan for power and contemplating suicide. Eventually, however, such people usually become part of one of the thousands of anonymous, dangerous cults ranging from two to perhaps one hundred members each, scattered and rapidly growing across this continent and beyond.

Satanism is a blatantly demonic religion, although not all Satanists adhere to a belief in the supernatural or a literal, personal Devil. Some Satanists are cynical atheists who see man as a self-centered animal in a universe with no inherent moral constraints. They see the figure of Satan as the mythical embodiment of a radical realism which says, "Hey, we know man is selfish. Let's put away the illusions of self-improvement foisted by man's religions and fulfill the self-centered freedom for which we were made."

Others may believe in a supernatural universe but see Satan as a figurative symbol for controlling universal forces through mind power. Yet most self-styled Satanists, once they advance past the novice stages, do apparently come to believe in and worship the literal Devil. They give everything to him, believing that he and his demons will overthrow God and usher in a reign of eternal self-gratifying evil.

Satan's Fishing Hooks

Fishing lures work on two principles: fascination and deception. Satanic lures are no different.

How does that bouncing baby boy, cooing in his bassinet, 14 or so years later end up slinking into a graveyard at midnight, cutting up animals as a sacrifice? According to Dr. Paul Carlin, an expert in satanic crimes and a consultant to law-enforcement agencies, every self-styled satanic cult has a three-step recruiting process: manipulation, intimidation, and domination.[7]

First, there is *manipulation*. Prospects are often intelligent but have a low self-image. They are impressionable, need to belong, and may be alienated from friends, church, or family. Within, they are deeply rebellious. Other traits common to those most vulnerable to satanic recruitment are these:

- A middle- to upper-class background
- Socially shy
- From a broken home
- A latchkey kid
- Susceptible to peer pressure
- Victim of prior sexual abuse
- Little parental involvement in his or her life
- Creative and curious
- Over- or under-achiever

At this moment the emphasis in recruiting is shifting to *church kids*. So if your child doesn't fit the traditional composite, don't stop reading.

Usually, recruiters offer free sex and drugs in a party atmosphere. Yet there are other satanic "hooks." Whether deliberately used by a recruiter or not, these reach into the depths of popular youth culture, floating innocently before potential victims. These victims become part of a large group that most researchers call the "thrill-seeking fringe" of self-styled Satanism. Most thrill-seekers are "good kids" who are being drawn into an evil game by one or more of the following enticements:

Fantasy role-playing games and fantasy comics. *Dungeons & Dragons* is the most notorious game. One author has described *Dungeons & Dragons* as "the most effective, most magnificently packaged, most profitably marketed, most thoroughly researched introduction to the occult in man's recorded history."[8] Yet other games abound, even in video format. Cashing in on the fantasy-occult jackpot, even comics by major publishers feature heroes and plots that exalt the demonic and are explicitly blasphemous of Jesus Christ and Christianity.

Ouija Board, tarot cards, and ESP. These are not innocent party games. The least that can happen to a child dabbling in these practices is bondage to superstition. The worst: demonic harassment and control. Yet in our day the net is spreading as even "1-900" phone numbers sell the occult to TV viewers 24 hours a day.

Horror movies and books. These forms of "entertainment" desensitize the conscience of a child toward murder, rebellion, and the occult. Some movies have gained a cult status, seen over and over again by a devoted audience. These movies are currently becoming a breeding ground for the growth of satanic recruiting networks.

Heavy-metal rock music. The suicide, sex, drugs, and violence that we have seen are part and parcel of the rock world and can culminate in overt Satanism. More about this shortly.

Party seances. Even Christian kids are getting involved in this. Dr. Neil Anderson of Biola University, an expert on demonic influence, told our audience about a game that researchers found common among 1725 Christian high school students in a recent survey. It was called "Bloody Mary."

This game "requires a child to go into a completely dark bathroom alone, spin around six times, face the mirror, and call upon Bloody Mary to show herself. In many cases these children, all high school age, reported they saw something that frightened them." Dr. Anderson went on to conclude, "There was no physical explanation for seeing something in a totally dark room. These kids have unwittingly opened themselves up to demonic powers."[9]

Obsession with martial arts. Sean Sellers was a student of the Ninja ethic, which draws upon Zen Buddhism and mind control. While not overtly satanic in itself, this discipline can be adapted to fit into a satanic view of life which ascribes utmost value to power, psychic discipline, and domination of others. In the wrong circumstances, your young "Ninja Turtle" could become a Ninja Devil.

Dressing in black and wearing occultic symbols. You can see them cruising the malls of every town in this country, often near the video game arcade and movie theater. Black clothes, either long or "punk" hairstyles, heavy-metal T-shirts. Confused, blinded, rebellious, and ripe for the picking.

Interest in pornography. A dehumanizing and desensitizing strategy. Many Satanists are involved in pornography or encourage it. Corruption of God's image and desecration of the mind of a young person go hand-in-hand in Satan's strategy.

Climbing the Devil's Ladder

According to Dr. Carlin, as the prospect is cultivated the pitch will be, "Nobody accepts you; we accept you. Nobody loves you; we love you. We offer you, the powerless, *immediate* power through the secret forces of darkness."

The initial manipulation phase continues when light rituals and chants bridge over to animal sacrifices. If a person accepts the killing, and is desensitized to it, he or she is deemed a good prospect for advancement. If not, he is shunned.

If he goes too far before rebelling against the group, the second phase, *intimidation*, is initiated. Usually this happens when perverted sex rituals and even necrophilia begin (unearthing dead bodies for ceremonies and perverted sex). The cult threatens to expose the reluctant recruit, or sacrifice him or a family member. "Examples" serve to keep others in line.

Eventually the recruit psychologically breaks to the point of *domination*, the final state. This is why even victims of kidnapping and molestation often stay with cults. The brainwashing is complete. Now the member is ready to commit almost any crime in the name of Satan.

"But It Doesn't Happen to Christian Kids"

In the recent survey by Neil Anderson of 1725 Christian teenagers, it was revealed that a fertile hunting ground for Satanism and the occult has become the *conservative* Christian school and youth group. Anderson reported that 70 percent of those surveyed heard "voices" which urged violence, suicide, or belief in heresy. Fifty percent have either seen or heard spirits they identified as evil. Twenty percent have had frequent thoughts of suicide; 24 percent had impulses to commit murder.[10]

The horrified Christian parents and teachers of these children pressed an investigation. They found that many of the Christian students were playing *Dungeons & Dragons* and dabbling into the occult—Ouija boards, Bloody Mary, and similar attractions. A majority of those engaged in *Dungeons & Dragons* were those now "hearing voices."

But would this really lead a Christian child into Satanism?

Ask the school counselor who gave this profile of the typical satanic dabbler to evangelist Steve Russo. "They're

all church kids," she stated, "They've had just enough...
of the supernatural to make them curious."[11] Or ask the
Texas parents of a Christian girl whose "new friends at
school" turned out to be Satanists.

After being deliberately manipulated, confused, and
finally turned against her parents, this pretty 17-year-
old was found staring lifelessly skyward in a cemetery
with a self-inflicted gunshot wound. At her funeral, her
satanic "friends" and their adult leaders told her parents *they* would be next, defiantly laying piles of black
roses on her coffin.[12]

Metal and Brimstone

Along with the myth that Christian children are
immune from satanic involvement is the assumption that
only the youth in the pressure cooker of big cities
are candidates for recruitment. Not long ago a young
woman from Bangor, Maine, wrote me with this unhappy
tale:

> My husband's 16-year-old sister was just a few
> months ago a professing Christian. She got
> mixed up with friends who listen to heavy
> metal and began listening to it herself. Now
> she tells me she wants to commit suicide,
> there's nothing to live for. I pleaded with her to
> remember what Christ did for her. She did not
> care. She said I had no way of knowing how
> bad hell is. She said, "I want to die. I want to go
> to hell."[13]

Heavy-metal music goes everywhere a Walkman
can take it—into big-city high schools and small-town
farms. And with it comes Satanism. In fact, satanic
worship is the logical culmination of everything I've
noted about heavy-metal rock 'n' roll in this book. Suicide, drugs, sex, violence, occultism—they all flow from

the same polluted stream and eventually come back to it.

It is unknown just how many rock groups are authentic Satan worshipers. Some of the occultic posturing is just a marketing ploy, designed to tap the reservoir of pent-up rebellion in youth culture. The evidence seems clear, however, that even the "pretend" bands are dupes for no-nonsense spiritual malfeasance.

Johanna Michaelson, an expert on the occult, reports that the Church of Satan has been promoting bands with satanic themes. The head of the Los Angeles branch of the church stated, "The groups are influencing the kids to come to Satan . . . even though they may deny it."[14] This fits with the assertion by a self-avowed satanic rock star that "most of [the bands] see the style as some sort of gimmick—they have no idea of the spiritual forces they're dealing with."[15]

But whether the groups are bona fide Satanists or not, their message, trappings, and mode of delivery are clearly of lower origin. As a parent, you're fighting three powerful forces involved in the selling of Satanism through music: 1) the ambience created by the symbolism, imagery, and concert settings; 2) the lyrics; and 3) the deliberate marketing strategies of the industry.

Imagery on album covers and publicity material reeks of Devil worship. Occult crime expert Pat Pulling cites a California probation officer describing the property of many of her most violent clients: "Illustrations of devils' heads, crucified figures, demonic babies, skeletons, pentagrams, black candles, and the occult number 666."[16] Upside-down crosses and parodies of significant biblical scenes and symbols are common fare. These are often found replicated on school notebooks and tattoos, and are even cut into the skin. Concerts frequently feature ritual torture, demonically clad musicians, and simulated sacrifice of animals, with plenty of blood and gore to go around.

Yet these only support even more horrific lyrics. For example, while Jesus Christ is a favorite target for ridicule in the rock music industry in general, the subtler slaps of lighter forms of rock music are now being replaced by the open blasphemy of performers such as King Diamond, who proclaims Jesus Christ to be "the deceiver." Another performer defiantly sings, "Jesus died for someone's sins, but not mine.... My sins are my own."[17] As Christ and Christianity are pressed underfoot, Lucifer is lifted up as a beacon to be worshiped and obeyed. In the song "Possessed," a band named Venom tells their young fans:

> Look at me, Satan's Child,
> Born of evil, thus defiled.
> Brought to life through satanic birth,
> Come look at me and
> I'll show you things that will open your eyes.
> Listen to me and I'll tell you things that will
> stick in your mind.[18]

"Come look at me ... listen to me...." The courtship of our sons and daughters is real. Are we as dedicated to keeping our children as the demonic realms are to stealing them?

Mission: Victory

Case 1: A 15-year-old boy is heavily engrossed in *Dungeons & Dragons,* heavy-metal rock, and the occult. His mother, alerted by these danger signs, finds a calendar where her son has picked a day for murdering his parents. She calls police, who find a loaded shotgun in his room. The boy is later led to Christ by a police officer.

Case 2: Ricky's mother, a Christian, attends a seminar on Satanism and becomes disturbed about her 13-year-old, formerly a model student. She finds that he is entering a private world of heavy-metal music, and

occultic symbols and poetry. When Ricky's uncle inter-
venes, the boy is lovingly confronted and quickly turns
around.[19]

Victories such as these can be won if adults are
aware of the dangers and know how to respond to them.
The difference between a Sean and a Ricky could be
someone like you.

Know the Broad Causes

The first step in shutting the door to Devil worship is
to acknowledge, and strategically counter, the impact of
the four social causes which set the stage for satanic
conversion. As I mentioned earlier in this chapter, these
are:

1. *A loss of faith in our society and its leaders.* Your
child needs to have leaders that he or she can have faith
in: you and your spouse, your adult friends, the leaders
of your church. You should point out prominent Christians and upstanding social leaders who serve as good
role models.

At the same time, your child needs to see that all
humans are fallible, and that evil and corruption are to
be expected in a fallen world. This is where the proper
worldview will be crucial, as explained in Chapter 2.
Ultimately, only God is perfect, and nothing except His
future regime on this planet will bring truly dependable
leadership to mankind. These are practical truths
which your children need to bask in as early as they can
appreciate them.

2. *Churches failing to exhibit the power of Christ.*
Make finding a better-than-average church an absolute
priority. Youth expert Jay Strack said in a "Point of
View" broadcast that he had moved his family halfway
across the country because he found a church with
dynamic, faithful preaching and a youth program with
spiritual life. Most people don't have the opportunity to

go to such lengths as a cross-country move, but as Jay said, "You *can* find the best church in your area." Don't settle for less.

Again, the counterbalance to a less-than-ideal church is *you*. Make yourself proficient in the Bible. This may take some effort, but good discipleship programs abound. If your church doesn't have one, find one through the radio or parachurch ministries.

Then start teaching God's Word to your children, including the reality of our conflict with Satan. Paul Carlin says that churches have lost, and need to recapture, the reality of the supernatural spiritual war portrayed in Scripture. Yet access to the Bible's key principles is easily available to parents and children! Neil Anderson tells of a young boy being drawn into Satanic oppression at age ten. His father spotted the signs of depression and irrational fear, and took his son on a walk during which he discussed with him his identity in Christ and the principles of spiritual combat as outlined in Ephesians 6. The father commented: "Have you ever wondered if a ten-year-old boy can relate to this material? He was all ears!...From that moment Matthew was a different boy. His whole countenance changed. The depression lifted immediately. His fear at night gradually disappeared as he began standing against Satan in Jesus' name. I believe Matthew now knows what it means to be a child of God."[20]

I'm amazed at how many people will take the time, effort, and money to protect their family against all kinds of physical hazards, but ignore the spiritual dangers which are much more serious. Let your children see the power of God shaping and refining you, warts and all, into an obedient, loyal, joyful servant of Christ. Know the Bible, believe it, and obey it—whether or not other Christians do the same. The chances are good that your children will make the decision to follow your example.

3. *Broken family relationships, including lack of unconditional love wedded to discipline and guidance.* The threat of Satanism makes the advice on home life mentioned throughout this book even more important. There are other excellent resources available, but the most important ingredient is to see the dangers of *not* paying attention to your family, and to make the conscious decision to guard your home and family relationships as if they were a mountain of gold.

4. *Widespread immorality and praise of evil, including occultism in school curricula.* Behavior and ideology affect each other. One of the chief tenets of formal Satanism is "Do what thou wilt." If immorality is not guarded against, the result may be more than a child who is merely an alcoholic; it could well be a son or daughter devoted to worshiping the Devil.

Be Alert to the Hooks

Review the hooks used to lure youth into the thrill-seeking fringe. Again, use practical and biblical admonitions attacking occultism and Satanism.

This is where you need to take up-front action as a parent. You need to immerse your child with the biblical worldview, so that he or she will not wish to be involved with any of these lures. This is a time to reason with your child, but it is not the time to pull punches. Let him know how seriously God takes these matters, and how seriously you take them as well.

Occultic involvement in any of the activities listed in this chapter should be unconditionally off-limits. Further, you should urge your child to report any signs of this in his friends to you, especially if it is in a church group.

Remember also that when churched children are infiltrated with thrill-seeking Satanism, they are often introduced into it by another churched child. That's why you need to make it a major priority to make your pastor or youth pastor aware of videos such as *Hell's Bells* (Reel to Real Ministries) or *Devil Worship in America* (Jeremiah Films), and urge them to show these to the youth group. It is *crucial* to bring these subjects out in the open with churched youth. I guarantee you'll be surprised at what you find out!

You Are the Link

Accounts of the tragedies caused by Satanism become all the more tragic when you read words like those of the mother of Pete Roland, a high school student who beat his friend Steve Newberry to death with a baseball bat as a sacrifice to Satan. She said, "I saw the satanic symbols in his book work.... I assumed it was a passing phase.... I would advise anybody, if they see anything like that, to look into it, don't ignore it. It doesn't pass...."[21]

A nosy parent is often a good parent. When danger signs are spotted, *get involved*. When they are confirmed, *get more involved*! Do research and seek counsel. Pray constantly and take seriously the spiritual warfare described in Ephesians 6. Then lovingly confront the victim about the propriety of his or her activities.

You can use the same tactics and resources I just suggested for preempting satanic dabbling, except that this time the focus will be on *correction*. But you must do your homework, both to detect and react to the crisis. If intervention at this level doesn't work, then professional help may be needed.

Of course, the best offense is a good defense: a home where a Christian worldview is taught and lived out, and a church where God's Word is preached and His power is evident in lives. Yet apart from alert adults, even this may not be enough. *You* are the ultimate link.

RESOURCES

Books:

The Devil's Web, by Pat Pulling

Satanism in America, by Michael Haynes and Pal Carlin (Michael Paul and Associates, Crockett, Texas)

Video:

Devil Worship: The Rise of Satanism (Jeremiah Films)

Part
Four

FINISHING
WELL

CHAPTER SEVENTEEN

Am I My Nephew's Keeper?

This book began with a warning that children in America have become targets. A variety of people in command of vast fortunes are seeking to control your child's mind, body, and future. Their values are often diametrically opposed to yours. If they succeed, the results are likely to be disastrous.

But what about other parents' children? Don't we have an obligation to help them too? Perhaps more to the point, can we hope to succeed in protecting our own kids if we do *nothing* to fight the danger to others? Our children grow up in a world that impacts their lives. If we expect them to grow the right way, then we must impact that world—for the sake of other parents' children as well as our own.

There are several steps you can take to impact the surrounding culture. You won't be able to do all or perhaps even most of them, so don't burn yourself out trying. The key is that you *can do some of them*. If every

Christian parent did at least one or two, the combined effect on our world would be extraordinary.

So pick out a cause or project and become an agent for change in your society, because that's what being "salt" and "light" is all about (Matthew 5:13-16). Leave your individual mark on history by getting involved where you are. The beneficiaries will be your own children, the children of your neighbors, and your country.

Here are seven steps to get you started.

1. Educate Yourself

Trends and events in politics and the general culture make a difference in the lives of children, and that fact alone should spur you on to learn more about what the world has in mind for our sons and daughters.

How can you educate yourself? First, pay some attention to the newspapers, TV, and radio, but take what they say with a grain of salt. The problem is that with today's media, bias toward moral and political liberalism is rampant. Yet they accomplish their agenda with style; the deceptions are most dangerous because they are made to appear very *believable*. That's why it's absolutely essential to get plugged into the growing field of alternate news sources.

News reporting and analysis which filters out the liberal bias is now available on radio and TV (usually Christian media outlets). Sometimes it is simply objective reporting, and sometimes commentary and analysis from a Christian or conservative standpoint.

The best of the alternate media practice truth in advertising by clearly letting you know when they are giving editorial opinion versus straight reporting of facts—a distinction which the liberal media don't often give you.

Beyond these day-to-day sources, make it a point to read at least one or two good books a year about current issues, and how a Christian worldview applies to them.

What issues should you know about? Certainly the 12 battles for children discussed in this book would deserve attention. Issues frequently in the news include: abortion, educational policy, economics (will we keep moving toward a bigger, more intrusive, more expensive government?), foreign affairs, political reform, moral issues such as homosexual rights, AIDS, and crime.

We live in an increasingly interconnected world in which all these issues have a bearing on the raising of your children and the kind of world they will live in, so you need to apply a biblical mindset to as many of these as you can.

2. Educate Others

Share what you learn, and make your sources available to people you know. I've found that Americans are usually more receptive than you might think to what others have to say and where to get good information.

It's especially vital to educate those who may be passive, but who could be transformed if only they knew the facts. One woman wrote to me saying:

> I had more or less closed myself off in my own little world. I had never even realized the changes that had taken place, the things that were really happening even in my own state, in my own community....I am no longer a sleeping Christian...not just listening, but also applying [God's Word] to my life....I am sharing with my friends, especially the passive ones, who tend to close their eyes to what's going on in this world.

One tip: Begin to share with those who are more likely to be receptive. Conflict shouldn't be feared, but in terms of cost effectiveness you should save the jousting with your pro-abortion Uncle Jack for your spare time.

3. Use the Incredible Gift of the Ballot

God commands us to pray for rulers so that the culture will be open to allowing the gospel to be preached and Christianity to saturate the population (1 Timothy 2:1-4). If we are to pray for leaders who won't threaten to persecute our faith and institute the spiritual subversion of our children, isn't it the height of hypocrisy not to *vote* for such leaders as well?

When I was growing up, I remember many preachers from various denominations saying that it was a sin to vote. Considering the spiritual damage done by the humanists who gladly rushed in to fill the vacuum, the decision to withdraw from the political arena was tragic. Rather than being biblical, it was instead a self-righteous *imitation* of spirituality. And sadly, the ones who are likely to pay the price are our children. In the past few years elected officials have taxed homemakers out of homes and into the marketplace (and their babies into day-care centers), funded the mass execution of millions of children through abortion, halted the appointment of decent judges on the ground that they were Christians, and generally contributed to the erosion of our social fabric.

God cared very much about who was elected to lead our country. By His grace alone He gave us a land where we can use the vote as a tool of stewardship to influence the culture in the best interests of the children who will be impacted by it. God cared, but all too often Christians have not. And it is often the children who suffer. Now the time has come to admit our mistakes and do our duty. As a parent, you need to be one of those leading the way. How do you get started?

First, develop a biblical view on the main issues. Read some appropriate books and network with Christians already involved and knowledgeable. Decide your "nonnegotiables" (I personally would have a hard time voting for anyone who was "pro-choice" regarding abortion), and then decide what you are willing to compromise.

Second, learn where the various candidates stand on the key issues. Call their headquarters if necessary. If you don't get a straight answer, you need to be suspicious. I would suggest this even for candidates at the lowest levels, such as county commissioner or school board, since this is where most congressmen get their start. And of course, positions like the school board have an obvious bearing on the lives of children all around you.

Third, if you can, volunteer for a candidate in a strategic race. Make phone calls, walk precincts, stuff envelopes, give money...whatever you can do. Your influence can be greater than you think.

A few years ago, one of the most successful pro-family state legislators in the country, Penny Pullen of Illinois, was reelected by only *16 votes* after demanding a recount of the original tally, which had shown her losing. It was that close. In 1976 the President of the United States was unseated by an average of less than a few votes per precinct. Your vote and your influence could help make the difference in the laws that govern your city, county, state, and nation. In fact, your *failure to vote* will make a difference also—and not one you may want to live with.

4. Develop the Fine Art of Cage-Rattling

Although our political system is hardly perfect, it is still true that the ship of state is driven by the winds of public pressure. Not only is political action generated by grass-roots activism and people speaking out, but other intangible factors in our culture are also influenced by the voice of opinion.

Think of it this way: Three or four column inches of space in a newspaper may be sold to advertisers for several hundred dollars per day. In magazines, the price goes up. Why? Simply because more people read it, and people's minds and actions are changed by what they read.

Yet there are bright, articulate parents who would love to have hundreds of dollars to spend on ad space to express their ideas who *never* write a letter to the editor. They also *never* call a radio talk-show to take advantage of free time that advertisers are paying top dollar to obtain.

Letters don't have to be literary masterpieces—just well-reasoned and legible. Phone calls don't need to be polished speeches—just well-reasoned and audible. Religious jargon should be kept under cover or "translated" into words that everyone can understand. Our views should be strong, but not strident. Challenging, but never obnoxious.

Christians today need to *communicate* their ideas with the world. The public, the press, politicians, and opinion-shapers need to know what we're thinking. It does make a difference.

5. Personally Challenge Threats to Children

It's amazing what the simple actions of just one person will do. Jerry Kirk of Cincinnati (President of the National Coalition Against Pornography, or N-CAP) tells of seeing soft-core pornographic magazines at a favorite gas station near his home.

He began by politely complaining to the station manager. That afternoon he called the district and regional managers for the large oil company that owned the station. Within a few minutes he was speaking to the corporate president's office. By the end of the week all pornographic material was removed from his corner station—and every other station of that brand in America. Not bad for an afternoon's work!

Another example of victory waiting to happen is the curtailing of harmful television. Complain by phone or letter to local television station managers and to the networks. Often these managers have told "Point of View" listeners that a few calls either way have made the difference about whether to air or preempt sexually borderline programs. Also, complain to advertisers; this is a proven method for getting action.

One caller to my talk show recounted how she saw a highly objectionable television program and called the local station. The station manager had told her that he had some major doubts about the propriety of the program, but that 13 people had called or written with positive comments about a similar show aired previously. He said that if they had received *just a few* negative calls or letters, they would have pulled the program off!

"Just a few calls or letters." I firmly believe that's how close we are to scuttling many lewd programs, even at the network level.

Contrary to popular opinion, we *can* make a difference by becoming involved. The only question is, *will we?*

6. Narrow Your Focus and Concentrate Your Fire

Adopt one or two issues close to your heart and concentrate on them (while of course keeping an eye on the others).

One excellent example that allows parents to do this is Citizens for Excellence in Education, based in Costa Mesa, California. CEE is a Christian network with state and local branches that organizes parents to protect their children from humanistic abuse in the public schools.

In 1990, CEE spearheaded a parents' revolt when it was discovered that the Los Angeles County School District was introducing a pilot program called "Mission

S.O.A.R." (Set Objectives Achieve Results). Sold as an anti-gang "self-esteem" program, it was found to be a thinly veiled adaptation of a textbook for self-hypnosis and channeling spirit guides!

The Pennsylvania CEE publishes a highly informative monthly booklet for members which keeps them rallied against month-to-month attempts to manipulate children according to values-free educational tactics.

Your calling might be education, in which case you might want to research the issues and join a group like CEE; or it might be pornography, in which case you could join N-CAP. Whatever your specialty, it's important for parents and adults to plug in and optimize the limited, but valuable, time which God has granted them.

7. Love Your Neighbor's Children As Your Own

In 1984, during the crest of the Christian political reawakening, Richard Cizik wrote a book entitled *The High Cost of Indifference: Can Christians Afford Not to Act?*

Today, Christian parents are beginning to discover the cost of indifference: their children. Indifferent no more, many of them are not only putting their homes in order, but they are coming out of the homes and helping straighten out our society.

It will not be easy, but it will not be impossible either. Since 1980, Christians have learned that helping elect a President was good, but not sufficient. Now that the glamour has worn off, a growing core are rolling up their sleeves and making an impact at the grass-roots level in their school districts and town councils.

These parents of the 90's are not only learning what it means to be their brother's keeper, but the keeper of their brother's children as well. As the Golden Rule implies, helping others is the best way to help yourself, and in this case the "others" may be your own children

CHAPTER EIGHTEEN

Rehab for Wounded Parents

Several types of parents will read this book. One type is comprised of those parents whose children have fallen prey to one or more of the threats described here, and are roasting themselves over the flames of guilt, wondering what they could have done differently.

This chapter is for them.

What do parents do when their children fail them? What do they do when *they* fail their children? Because we live in a world of failure, these are questions that must be met head-on. Here are six principles that are crucial to meeting this ultimate worry.

1. Don't heap unnecessary blame on yourself, or assume responsibility for the sins of others.

This may seem unusual advice from a book whose premise is that parents need to reclaim ownership of their children's destiny through knowing and meeting the key threats of our time. Yet everything that you can do is under the greater umbrella of certain facts over which you have no control at all.

First, your child has a free will, and is accountable to God for his own actions. You can *influence* your child's life, but you cannot *determine* it; that is his or her responsibility alone.

Remember what I said in the chapter on homosexuality: Certain family factors can predispose many homosexuals toward the path they eventually take. Perhaps a father was too distant and too absorbed in his work to be a strong male role model. But this is a far cry from saying that a homosexual could never have resisted the effect of those circumstances. In fact, in every case the mistakes of the parents could have been overcome by the son or daughter.

As a parent, it's fair to take responsibility for what you did wrong. But to take responsibility for the wrongs of others, even your own children, is going too far. As Joe Dallas writes, "It is the fallen nature, not parental shortcomings, which is ultimately the cause of all dysfunction, sin, and perversion. To assume responsibility for an adult child's sin is to assume a certain omnipotence. And clearly, whatever else we may be, parents are not omnipotent." [1]

But let's even take it a step farther. This principle is not only true for the sins of your child, but also for those of the predators roaming our society who seek to destroy our children. Of course, every parent must do what he or she can to protect, prepare, or reclaim his children. But what if he or she falls short in this task? Should he be exiled to a purgatory of self-guilt and wondering "what if"? I think not. We are in a fight for our children against cunning and often well-financed aggressors. Parents, including good ones, will not always win this struggle. If this describes you, then I think it's essential for you to realize that the true blame falls on the shoulders of the enemy, not on yours.

2. If your child is wayward, don't reject him or "ex-communicate" him.

One of the most direct pathways to your own healing is the unconditional love you can give your son or daughter when it would seem most reasonable for you to reject him in bitterness and pain. You don't have to condone his actions, but to reject him *personally* is to reject a part of you and your life. And most tragically, an angry backlash will threaten to cut off lines of communication which are vital to your child's restoration.

3. Take care of yourself.

You can't control what has happened in the past, and you can't control the decisions of others. Nevertheless, you *can* control your own reactions and your own future. Self-blame and retribution are methods of "excommunicating" yourself—something which God Himself has not done to you. Instead, you need to continue to attend to your own spiritual growth by confessing any legitimate sins you have committed, being frank with God about any true shortcomings, and then moving on toward letting God control your life through the Scriptures, prayer, and fellowship with other imperfect Christians. The man who called himself "the chief of sinners" said that he was continually "forgetting what is behind and straining toward what is ahead" (Philippians 3:13). Whatever has occurred with your children, God still wants to know you better and utilize you more, and He has the transforming ability to do just that.

4. Find others who can support you.

Silent agony is often the most convenient way to handle the grief of a wayward son or daughter, yet it is a dead-end street that God intends you to avoid. That's one of the reasons He created the church. Churches were never meant to be country clubs or etiquette societies with steeples and pews. Someone has said that churches should be hospitals where patients heal each other. Failure to confide in a good friend, relative, or support group who can sympathize and encourage you in the right direction is not only a disservice to yourself, but to those whom God has provided to help you. If you can't find that support in your own church, contact one of the parachurch ministries we have suggested in the *Further Help* section or from your own references. Not only will you find help there, but you will be able to help others as well.

5. Don't try to repair things that you have no power over, especially your child's attitudes.

There are points where you must acknowledge God's control and your children's choices (especially when they reach adulthood), and then relinquish them to His will. Of course you will be concerned, worried, fearful, or sorrowful, and often it would be highly unnatural if you weren't. Yet how will you direct all that energy? There is a limit to the amount of influence you can have on another person, including your child. After you have done what you can, talking with good friends and counselors and depending upon the weapon of prayer are all that is left. And often these are better alternatives than any others.

6. Remember that God can heal.

Have you ever wondered what was going through the mind of the father (and mother) of the prodigal son before the son saw the error of his ways and returned home? Perhaps the father condemned himself for being too permissive, for not guarding against the glittering temptations of the world which lured his foolish boy away. Perhaps he spent hours in imaginary debate with his son over issues that had driven them apart. Maybe he doubted or even railed at God for allowing the delinquency to occur.

And he was undoubtedly embarrassed. Perhaps he withdrew to his home, not up to facing his friends. Did he ever try to locate his son, or talk him back into the house?

The truth is that we don't know; he may have resorted to all of these things or none of them. What we *do* know is that when his son was ready to return, dad was running down the road with open arms, ready to receive him back. His love was unconditional, and I suspect that his son's return was in answer to many nights of fervent prayer. And, most importantly, I believe that the love, prayers, and trust in God would have been a part of the father's life even if the prodigal son had never returned.

It's the same today. We may live in a shooting gallery where wounds are frequent, but God's grace is still sufficient to heal, once we are open to receiving it from Him.

Further Help

Here is a listing of books, videos, and organizations that cover more than one of the specific areas considered in this book. For those that do zero in on specific areas, see the close of the pertinent chapter. The books and videos can be obtained or ordered at most local Christian bookstores.

Books

A Parent's Survival Guide to the Public Schools, by Sally Reed

The Big Book of Home Learning, by Mary Pride

The Christian Home School, by Gregg Harris

Home School Burnout, by Raymond and Dorothy Moore

Like Lambs to the Slaughter: Your Child and the Occult, by Johanna Michaelsen

New Age Masquerade: The Hidden Agenda in Your Child's Classroom, by Eric Buehrer

Raising Worldly-Wise but Innocent Kids, by David Wyrtzen

Ravaged by the New Age: Satan's Plan to Destroy Our Kids, by Texe Marrs

Saturday Morning Mind Control, by Phil Phillips

The Seduction of Our Children, by Neil T. Anderson and Steve Russo

Trial and Error: The American Civil Liberties Union and Its Impact on Your Family, by George Grant

What Are They Teaching Our Children? (What You Can Do About Humanism and Textbooks in Today's Public Schools, by Mel and Norma Gabler

Your Child and the New Age, by Berit Kjos

Videos

Hell's Bells (Reel to Real Ministries)

All Rapped Up (Reel to Real Ministries)

Gods of the New Age (Jeremiah Films)

Devil Worship: The Rise of Satanism (Jeremiah Films)

Halloween Trick or Treat (Jeremiah Films)

The Evolution Conspiracy (Jeremiah Films)

Alternative entertainment for children:

The Donut Hole (Gospel Light Films)

The Amazing Children, The Amazing Book, The Music Machine, The Amazing Miracles, Benny's Biggest Battle (Agapeland Videos)

Organizations

American Family Association. 107 Parkgate, P.O. Drawer 2440, Tupelo, MS 38803. Provides public information on political action against indecency, obscenity, and blasphemy in the culture, especially entertainment and the arts. Publishes monthly newsletter and timely action alerts.

Further Help 265

Christian Research Institute. P.O. Box 500, San Juan Capistrano, CA 92693. Research on cults and the occult available to individuals.

Citizens for Excellence in Education. P.O. Box 3200, Costa Mesa, CA 92628. A national organization, with local branches, dedicated to helping parents of children in public schools who are dealing with values clarification, New Age practices, and other anti-Christian influences.

Concerned Women for America. P.O. Box 65453, Washington D.C. 20035-5453. The nation's largest women's organization, CWA lobbies for traditional values and informs its members through newsletters, radio programs, and meetings. Has local groups.

Eagle Forum. P.O. Box 618, Alton, IL. National women's organization with local chapters committed to defending traditional values in government through education and legislative action.

Family Research Council. 700 13th Street NW, Suite 500, Washington D.C. 20005. Research and public information on laws that affect the family.

Moms-in-Touch. P.O. Box 1120, Poway, CA 92074. A network of thousands of mothers who meet weekly to pray for their children, their children's teachers, principals, and other local school officials.

National Council for Better Education. 101 N. Alfred Street, Alexandria, VA 22314. Information to parents and legislators on the effects of humanistic education in public education.

Parents' Music Resource Center. 1500 Arlington Blvd., Ste. 300, Arlington, VA 22209. Provides up-to-date public information on destructive entertainment, especially rock lyrics.

Probe Ministries. 1900 Firman Dr., Richardson, TX 75081. Applies Christian worldview to academic disciplines from high school to university levels.

Rutherford Institute. P.O. Box 7482, Charlottesville, VA 22906-7482. A national network of practicing attorneys committed to defending those whose religious rights have been violated, and pushing for laws protecting those rights.

Spiritual Counterfeits Project. P.O. Box 4308, Berkeley, CA 94704. Provides information on cults and the occult, including New Age.

Summit Ministries. P.O. Box 207, Manitou Springs, CO 80829. Brief but intensive college prep courses in Christian worldview thought and morals.

Watchman Fellowship. P.O. Box 13251, Arlington, TX 76094. Research on cults, the occult, world religions, and New Age influence in society.

Appendix

Model Hatch Amendment Letter

Parent's name _____

Address _____

City, State _____

    I am the parent of _____ ,

who attends _____
school. Under U.S. legislation and court decision, parents have the primary responsibility for their children's education, and pupils have certain rights which the schools may not deny.

    Parents have the right to be assured that their children's beliefs and moral values are not undermined by the schools. Pupils have their right to have and to hold their values and moral standards without direct or indirect manipulations by the schools through the curricula, textbooks, audiovisual materials, or supplementary assignments.

Under the Hatch Amendment, I hereby request that my child not be involved in any school activities or given material listed below unless I have first reviewed all the relevant materials and have given my written consent for their use:

Psychological and psychiatric treatment that is designed to affect behavioral, emotional, or attitudinal characteristics or is designed to elicit information about attitudes, habits, traits, opinions, beliefs, or feelings of an individual or group;

Values clarification, use of moral dilemmas, discussion of religious or moral standards, role-playing or open-ended discussions of situations involving moral issues, and survival games, including life-death decision exercises;

Contrived incidents for self-revelation; sensitivity training, group encounter sessions, talk-ins, magic circle techniques, self-evaluation, and auto-criticism; strategies designed for self-disclosure, including the keeping of a diary, journal, or log book;

Sociograms or sociodrama; psychodrama; blindfolded walks; isolation techniques;

Death education, including topics of abortion, euthanasia, suicide, use of violence, and discussions of death and dying;

Nuclear war, nuclear policy, and nuclear classroom games;

Globalism, one-world government, or antinationalistic curricula;

Discussion and testing on interpersonal relationships; discussions of attitudes toward parents and parenting;

Educating in human sexuality, including premarital sex, extramarital sex, contraception, abortion, homosexuality, group sex and marriages, prostitution, incest, bestiality, masturbation, divorce, population control, and roles of males and females; sex behavior and attitudes of student and family;

Pornography and any materials containing profanity and/or sexual explicitness;

Guided-fantasy techniques; hypnotic techniques; imagery and suggestology;

Organic evolution, including Darwin's theory;

Discussions of witchcraft, occultism, the supernatural, and Eastern mysticism;

Political and/or religious affiliations of students or family;

Income of family;

Nonacademic personality tests; questionnaires or personal and family life attitudes.

The purpose of this letter is to preserve my child's rights under the Protection of Pupil Rights Amendment (the Hatch Amendment) to the General Education Provision Act, and under its regulations as published in the Federal Register of September 6, 1984, which became effective November 12, 1984.

These regulations provide a procedure for filing complaints first at the social level, and then with the U.S. Department of Education. If a voluntary remedy fails, federal funds can be withdrawn from those in violation of the law.

I respectfully ask you to send me a substantive response to this letter attaching a copy of your policy

statement on procedures for parental permission requirement, to notify all my child's teachers, and to keep a
copy of this letter in my child's permanent file.

Thank you for your cooperation.

Signed,

_____

Letter adapted from *How Good Is Your School?* by Sally D. Reed, founder of the National Council for Better Education, Washington D.C.

Notes

CHAPTER 1: The Future: Up for Grabs

1. Jacob Aranza, *More Rock, Country and Backward Masking Unmasked* (Lafayette, LA:Huntington House, 1985), p. 99.
2. Charles Colson, *Against the Night* (Ann Arbor: Servant, 1989), pp. 10-11.

CHAPTER 2: Winning the Deadliest Battle

1. *Reminisce* magazine (Greendale, WI), Premiere Collector's Edition, 1991, p. 61.

CHAPTER 3: Caution: Treachery at Work

1. Kerby Anderson, "Challenging Humanism in your Child's School," in *Freedom Club Report*, International Christian Media, Dallas, TX, June 1991, p. 7.
2. "Point of View" radio talk show, Mar. 19, 1992, first of a two-day interview with Sally Reed.

CHAPTER 4: Competitive Parents, Healthy Children

1. "Point of View," Aug. 26, 1991.
2. "Point of View," Sep. 27, 1989.
3. "Point of View," Nov. 29, 1991.
4. "Point of View," Jan. 7, 1992.

CHAPTER 5: America's New Barbarians

1. Dan Coats, "America's Youth: A Crisis of Character," in *Imprimis*, Sep. 1991 (Hillsdale, MI: Hillsdale College), p. 2.
2. "Hometown bands go where no Dallas bands have gone before," in *Dallas Life* magazine, July 31, 1988, p. 14.
3. *Newsweek*, Jan. 6, 1992, p. 11, quoting the Minnesota Vikings' Joey Browner.
4. Coats, "Youth," p. 2.
5. Colson, *Against*, p. 77.
6. Cited by Eric Holmberg of *Reel to Real Ministries* in "Point of View" program, Aug. 26, 1992.
7. Coats, "Youth," p. 3.
8. Related by W.R. Coulson on "Point of View," Jan. 20, 1992.
9. Christina Hoff Sommers, "Teaching the Virtues," in *Imprimis* (Hillsdale, MI: Hillsdale College), Nov. 1991, p. 3
10. Ibid.
11. Ibid., pp. 2-4.

CHAPTER 6: Why Johnny Can't Succeed

1. Quoted by Ronald Nash, *The Closing of the American Heart* (Dallas: Probe, 1990).
2. Sally D. Reed, *A Parent's Survival Guide to the Public Schools* (Alexandria, VA: National Council for Better Education, 1990), p. 201, citing John Dewey, "University Schools," in *University Records*, pp. 417-22.
3. Charles Colson, *Jubilee* Newsletter (Washington D.C.: Prison Fellowship, Feb. 1991).

CHAPTER 7: The Trap of "Safe Sex"

1. Ed Bark, "Doogie faces sexual rite of passage," in *Dallas Morning News*, Sep. 24, 1991, p. 1C.
2. "Student poll: drinking, sex par for many," in *Denver Post*, June 21, 1991, p. 1A.
3. "Messages not getting to teens," in *San Diego Union*, June 18, 1991, p. C3; also, congressional testimony by Kathleen Sullivan, director of Project Respect, June 17, 1991.
4. Ibid.
5. Ibid.
6. Interview with Shannen Doherty, *TV Guide*, Aug. 24, 1991, p. 9.
7. S. Robert Lichter, Linda S. Lichter, and Stanley Rothman, *Watching America* (New York: Prentice Hall, 1991), p. 48.
8. "Point of View," July 11, 1990.
9. "Messages" in *San Diego Union*, June, 18, 1991, p. C3.
10. George Grant, *Grand Illusions: The Legacy of Planned Parenthood* (Brentwood, TN: Wolgemuth & Hyatt, 1989), p. 108. This award-winning book should be read by every American parent.
11. Ibid., pp. 30-32.
12. "Point of View," Sep. 18, 1991.
13. Joe S. McIlhaney, *Safe Sex: A Doctor Examines the Realities of AIDS and Other STDs* (Grand Rapids: Baker, 1991), pp. 38-43. Also see Grant, *Illusions*, pp. 30-33.

CHAPTER 8: Why Gay Is Not Happy

1. Paul Cameron, *Exposing the AIDS Scandal* (Lafayette, LA: Huntington House, 1988), p. 34.
2. Joe Dallas, *Desires in Conflict* (Eugene, OR: Harvest House, 1991), p. 7.
3. As cited by Paul Cameron, *Exposing*, pp. 35-37.
4. "Sex, American Style: Trend to the Traditional," in *Los Angeles Times*, Feb. 19, 1990, p. A1; personal letter from Dr. Paul Cameron, Family Research Institute, Mar. 14, 1990; 1990 research summary by the Family Research Institute.
5. The most recent example was a small study done at the Salk Institute in La Jolla, California. A researcher claimed to have detected a difference in the size of a minute section of the brain when comparing homosexual and heterosexual cadavers. The study was touted on front pages nationwide. If homosexuals can prove a biological cause of their sexual preference, the theory goes, then they can claim the right to their behavior. So they ran this "finding" up the flagpole, and as always the media saluted.

   However, upon closer scrutiny, some serious problems with the study began to surface. First, the size of the sample of cadavers, 43 in all, was much too small to draw any meaningful conclusions. Second, another leading researcher pointed out that the study rather hastily presumed that the "heterosexual" cadavers were not gay. In fact, these "heterosexuals" had died of AIDS! The odds were therefore strong that they weren't all heterosexual, which would mean the comparison with the known homosexual cadavers would be meaningless. Even the researcher himself had to admit that he was working on presumption; and statistically, it was a very bad presumption to make. (See "Male homosexuality, brain structure linked," in *Dallas Morning News*, Aug. 30, 1991, p. 1A, and *Time* magazine, Sep. 9, 1991, p. 61).

6. Jerry and Steve Arterburn, *How Will I Tell My Mother?* (Nashville: Oliver Nelson, 1988), pp. 99-100.
7. Cameron, *Exposing*, pp. 149-52.
8. As reported in "Family Research: Newsletter of the Family Research Institute," Washington D.C., Oct.-Dec. 1988.

CHAPTER 9: The Madonna Strategy

1. From "The Second Coming," in *The Collected Poems of W.B. Yeats* (New York: MacMillan, 1956), p. 184.
2. Madonna interview, in *The Advocate*, May 7, 1991, p. 49; and as cited by Eric Holmberg in "Point of View," Aug. 26, 1991.
3. Thomas Jipping, *Heavy Metal, Rap, and America's Youth: Issues and Alternatives* (Washington, D.C.: Free Congress Foundation, 1990), p. 50.
4. "Point of View," Aug. 26, 1991.
5. Jipping, *Heavy Metal*, p. 46.
6. Ibid., p. 47.
7. Judith Reisman, *"Soft" Porn Plays Hardball* (Lafayette, LA: Huntington House, 1991), pp. 27-30,33,105-06.
8. "Point of View" interview with Alan Sears, Sep. 8, 1991.
9. Ibid.
10. Reisman, *Porn*, p. 13.
11. Ibid., p. 65.
12. Ibid.
13. Ibid., pp. 143-44.
14. Adapted from "Pornography: Extent and Evidence," by the National Coalition Against Pornography.
15. Reisman, *Porn*, pp. 98ff.
16. "Pornography Fact Sheet," by the National Coalition Against Pornography (NCAP), Cincinnati, Ohio.
17. "Pornography: Extent."
18. Ibid.
19. Family Research Institute study, "Child Molestation and Homosexuality" (Lincoln, NE/Washington D.C., 1987).
20. Rene Guyon, *The Ethics of Sex Acts*, 1948, as cited by Reisman, *Porn*, p. 37.
21. John Whitehead, *Parents' Rights* (Westchester, IL: Crossway, 1985), pp. 134-37.
22. Reisman, *Porn*, p. 152.

CHAPTER 10: The Party Generation

1. "Of Concern to Teens," in *USA Today*, June 25, 1991.
2. "Student Alcohol Abuse Up," in *Denver Post*, June 22, 1991, p. 1A.
3. Steve Arterburn and Jim Burns, *Drug-Proof Your Kids* (Pomona, CA: Focus on the Family, 1989), p. 108.
4. Ibid., p. 5.
5. Ibid, p. 23.
6. Felicity Barringer, "Alcohol Abuse Top Drug Problem Among Teenagers," in the *Sacramento Bee*, Sacramento, CA, p. B10.
7. Arterburn and Burns, *Drug-Proof*, p. 24.
8. Ibid., p. 25.
9. *Sacramento Bee*, op. cit.
10. Tipper Gore, *Raising PG Kids in an X-Rated Society* (Nashville: Abingdon, 1987), p. 135.
11. "Point of View," Sep. 5, 1990.

12. Cited by James Walker and Rick Branch, *The New Age in Our Schools* (Arlington, TX: Watchman Fellowship).
13. Arterburn and Burns, *Drug-Proof*, pp. 111-13.

CHAPTER 11: Fade to Black?

1. Metallica, "Fade to Black," in *Ride the Lightning* record album and lyrics, Elektra/ Asylum 60396-1. Written by Clifford Lee Burton, Lars Ulrich, Kirk L. Hammett, and James Allen Hetfield. Lyrics copyright 1984 by Creeping Death Music.
2. Terry Flynn, "Family Struggles to Understand Death," in *Cincinnati Enquirer,* June 20, 1991, citing Dr. Michael Sorter, child psychiatrist at Children's Hospital, University of Cincinnati Medical Center.
3. Kerby Anderson, "Teenage Suicide," in *Moody Monthly*, Feb. 1987, p. 19.
4. "Point of View," June 5, 1989.
5. Flynn, "Struggles."
6. Leslie Baldacci, "Despairing Teens Need Special Help," in *Chicago Sun-Times*, May 16, 1991, p. 5.
7. Gore, *PG Kids,* pp. 110-11, and Russ Wise, *Rock Speaks* (Richardson, TX: Probe Ministries, 1989), p. 2.
8. Baldacci, "Despairing."
9. "Parents fight..." in *Arizona Republic/Phoenix Gazette*, May 13, 1991, p. 2N6.
10. Baldacci, "Despairing," and many other sources.
11. "Point of View," July 11, 1990.
12. David Nicholson of Minirth-Meier Clinic in "Point of View," June 5, 1989.

CHAPTER 12: Cults: Rebellion into Religion

1. George Barna, *Marketing the Church* (Colorado Springs: NavPress, 1988), p. 22.
2. Cited by Caryl Matrisciana and Roger Oakland in *The Evolution Conspiracy* (Eugene: Harvest House, 1991) p. 25.
3. For a good defense of this teaching, I recommend *What You Need to Know About Jehovah's Witnesses*, by Lorri MacGregor (Harvest House), and *One on One with Jehovah's Witnesses*, by Christopher Corbett (Dallas: International Christian Media).
4. Timothy K. Jones, "Tracking America's Soul" (interview with George Gallup, Jr.), in *Christianity Today*, Nov. 17, 1989, p. 24.
5. Ed Gruss, ed., *We Left Jehovah's Witnesses* (Grand Rapids: Baker, 1975), pp. 102-03.
6. Ibid., p. 39.
7. Steven Hassan, *Combatting Cult Mind Control* (Rochester, VT: Park Street Press, 1988), pp. 48-49.
8. Ibid., p. 49.
9. 1 Thessalonians 5:21.
10. Steve Kemperman, *Lord of the Second Advent* (Ventura: Regal, 1981) (throughout narrative).
11. Hassan, *Mind Control*, p. 132.

CHAPTER 13: Training for a New World Order

1. Cited by Johanna Michaelsen, *Like Lambs to the Slaughter* (Eugene, OR: Harvest House, 1989), p. 24; also see B.K. Eakman, *Educating for the New World Order* (Portland: Halcyon House, 1991), p. 228.
2. Editorial by L. Brent Bozell in *USA Today*, Aug. 8, 1991, as cited in "The Five Minute Report" of the Council for National Policy, Aug. 9, 1991.
3. Ibid.
4. Whitehead, *Rights*, p. 113.
5. Robert Simonds, Sep. 1991 Report of the National Association of Christian Educators, Costa Mesa, CA, citing Bettina Dobbs, p. 2.

6. Phyllis Schlafly, *Child Abuse in the Classroom* (Westchester, IL: Crossway, 1988), p. 57.
7. Eakman, *Educating*, pp. 124-5.
8. Schlafly, *Abuse*, p. 137, cited by Berit Kjos, *Your Child and the New Age* (Wheaton: Victor, 1990), p. 46.
9. Mel and Norma Gabler, *What Are They Teaching Our Children?* (Wheaton: Victor, 1985), pp. 51-52.
10. Ibid., p. 48.
11. Ibid., pp. 47-64.
12. Eakman, *Educating*, pp. 12-13.
13. Kjos, *Child*, citing D. James Kennedy, *Train Up a Child* (Fort Lauderdale: Coral Ridge Ministries, a sermon delivered June 2, 1985).
14. Sally D. Reed, *A Parent's Survival Guide to the Public Schools* (Alexandria, VA: National Council for Better Education, 1991), p. 42.
15. Ibid., citing the high school civics text *United States Government: The People Decide*.
16. David Elkind, *The School Administrator*, June 1990, pp. 11,15.
17. Whitehead, *Rights*, pp. 58-61.

CHAPTER 14: Your Kids at God's Funeral

1. Carl Sagan, *Cosmos* (New York: Random House, 1980), p. 1.
2. Gabler, *Teaching*, p. 90.
3. Steven Galebach and Laura Millman, "Brief for Focus on the Family and Family Research Council As Amici Curiae in Support of Petitioners," in Lee v. Weisman (U.S. Supreme Court case # 90-1014), Oct. 1990.
4. "Student derided for biographical report on Jesus," in *Christian World Report*, Apr. 1991, p. 22.
5. John Whitehead, *The Second American Revolution* (Westchester, IL: Crossway, 1982), p. 52.
6. Francis Schaeffer and C. Everett Koop, *Whatever Happened to the Human Race?* (Old Tappan, NJ: Revell, 1979), p. 122.
7. Ibid, p. 124.
8. Ibid., p. 122.

CHAPTER 15: Godhood for Your Kids?

1. Tal Brooke, *When the World Will Be As One* (Eugene, OR: Harvest House, 1989), p. 113.
2. Ibid., p. 114.
3. Michaelson, *Lambs*, p. 113.
4. Brooke, *World*, p. 104.
5. Russell Chandler, *Understanding the New Age* (Dallas: Word, 1988), p. 154.
6. President's Special Report, National Association for Christian Educators/Citizens for Excellence in Education, Costa Mesa, CA, May 15, 1990.
7. "Children learn to tame grown-up stress," in *Eagle*, Bryan-College Station, TX, May 15, 1991, p. 1A.
8. Jack Canfield and Paula Klimeck, *New Age Magazine*, Feb. 1978, p. 28.
9. Dick Sutphen, *What Is*, Summer, 1986, p. 14.
10. For an excellent analysis of the *Impressions* series, see the work by Deborah Mendenhall for Focus on the Family.

CHAPTER 16: Things That Go Bump in the Night

1. Michael Haynes and Paul Carlin, *Satanism in America: What They Do Not Want You to Know* (Crockett, TX: Kerusso Company, Inc., 1989), p. 37. This is a law enforcement manual to satanic-related crime.
2. Pat Pulling, *The Devil's Web* (Fayetteville: Huntington House, 1989), p. 92.

3. Carlin and Haynes, *Satanism*, p. 37.
4. "Point of View" interview with Paul Carlin, July 23, 1991.
5. Accumulated from interviews with Johanna Michaelson, Carl Rasche, Pat Pulling, Paul Carlin, Charles Evans, and Mike Warnke.
6. The trilevel structure of Satanism was developed by Michael Paul & Associates, of Crockett, Texas, a law-enforcement consultant. See Carlin and Haynes, *Satanism*, and "Point of View," July 23, 1991.
7. Carlin interview, July 23, 1991.
8. Cited in Carlin and Haynes, *Satanism*, p. 16.
9. Neil Anderson and Steve Russo, *The Seduction of Our Children* (Eugene, OR: Harvest House, 1991), pp. 33ff.
10. Ibid.
11. Ibid., p. 103.
12. "Demonic Deception and Our Kids," audio tape, The Art of Family Living, Dallas, TX, 1991.
13. Letter on file, Nov. 23, 1990.
14. Cited in Michaelsen, *Lambs*, p. 267.
15. Ibid.
16. Pulling, *Web* p. 104.
17. From the video *Hell's Bells*, Reel to Real Ministries, Gainesville, FL, 1990.
18. Jipping, "Heavy Metal," p. 59.
19. Pulling, *Web*, pp. 140-41.
20. Anderson and Russo, *Seduction*, p. 108.
21. Michaelsen, *Lambs*, p. 274.

CHAPTER 18: Rehab for Wounded Parents

1. Dallas, *Desires*, p. 240.

Other Good
Harvest House Reading

THE SEDUCTION OF OUR CHILDREN
by *Neil T. Anderson and Steve Russo*

A battle is raging for the minds of our children. New age thinking has infiltrated our schools. Satanism is on the rise. Drugs and occultic music are everywhere. Neil Anderson, noted author of the bestselling book *The Bondage Breaker,* and international evangelist Steve Russo help equip parents to meet the growing spiritual assault against their children and family head-on, providing strategies to overcome the spiritual conflicts young people face.

GETTING THE BEST OUT OF YOUR KIDS*
by *Kevin Leman*

Dr. Kevin Leman offers solutions to the toughest problems parents face. From knowing when to send little ones to nursery school to guiding turbulent teens through the pressures of drugs and sex, Leman provides penetrating insight and time-tested advice on raising kids from start to finish.

LIKE LAMBS TO THE SLAUGHTER—
Your Child and the Occult
by *Johanna Michaelsen*

Dungeons and Dragons, Saturday morning cartoons, Star Wars, E.T., yoga, spirit guides, guided imagery and visualization, storybooks on witchcraft and the occult. This book explores basics of the New Age Movement as it relates to children and exposes the deadly effects of the subtle occult practices so prevalent among our youth today.

TOO OLD, TOO SOON
by *Doug Fields*

Too Old, Too Soon examines the changes to childhood brought about by a culture caught in overdrive and offers concrete suggestions parents can use to avoid the pitfalls of rushing their children to adulthood.

Dear Reader:

We would appreciate hearing from you regarding this Harvest House nonfiction book. It will enable us to continue to give you the best in Christian publishing.

1. What most influenced you to purchase *What Worries Parents Most?*
   - ☐ Author
   - ☐ Subject matter
   - ☐ Backcover copy
   - ☐ Recommendations
   - ☐ Cover/Title
   - ☐ _____

2. Where did you purchase this book?
   - ☐ Christian bookstore
   - ☐ General bookstore
   - ☐ Department store
   - ☐ Grocery store
   - ☐ Other

3. Your overall rating of this book:
   ☐ Excellent ☐ Very good ☐ Good ☐ Fair ☐ Poor

4. How likely would you be to purchase other books by this author?
   - ☐ Very likely
   - ☐ Somewhat likely
   - ☐ Not very likely
   - ☐ Not at all

5. What types of books most interest you?
   (check all that apply)
   - ☐ Women's Books
   - ☐ Marriage Books
   - ☐ Current Issues
   - ☐ Self Help/Psychology
   - ☐ Bible Studies
   - ☐ Fiction
   - ☐ Biographies
   - ☐ Children's Books
   - ☐ Youth Books
   - ☐ Other _____

6. Please check the box next to your age group.
   - ☐ Under 18
   - ☐ 18-24
   - ☐ 25-34
   - ☐ 35-44
   - ☐ 45-54
   - ☐ 55 and over

Mail to: Editorial Director
Harvest House Publishers
1075 Arrowsmith
Eugene, OR 97402

Name _____

Address _____

City _____ State _____ Zip _____

**Thank you for helping us to help you
in future publications!**